BUSINESS
BUZZWORDS

The Tough New Jargon of Modern Business

BUSINESS BUZZWORDS

The Tough New Jargon of Modern Business

MICHAEL JOHNSON

Basil Blackwell

First published 1990

Basil Blackwell Ltd
108 Cowley Road, Oxford, OX4 1JF, UK

Basil Blackwell Inc.
3 Cambridge Center
Cambridge, Massachusetts 02142, USA

British Library Cataloguing in Publication Data
A CIP catalogue record for this book is available from
the British Library

Library of Congress Cataloging in Publication Data
Johnson, Michael.
Business buzzwords: the tough new jargon of modern business/
Michael Johnson
ISBN 0–631–17107-X
1. Business–Dictionaries.   2. English language–Jargon.
I. Title.
HF 1001. J64 1990
650'.014–dc20   89–28288 CIP

Typeset in 11½ on 13½pt Palatino
by Eta Services (Typesetters) Ltd, Beccles, Suffolk
Printed in Great Britain by
T. J. Press Ltd, Padstow, Cornwall

CONTENTS

ACKNOWLEDGEMENTS

It took two years of constant screening and occasional hard work to compile the contents of this book. The most difficult part was keeping track of scraps of paper on which I had scrawled such linguistic curiosities as 'couch potato' or 'Gorbasm', to be later defined and entered into the growing list. Besides filtering out oddities from the speech and writing of business executives, I depended on the help of a network of friends and colleagues who took an interest in this effort.

First and foremost among the helpers was my wife, Jacqueline, who ploughed through several jargon-riddled business books hunting for material. The takings seemed to be in inverse proportion to the value of the book, making the chore less than a happy one. Perhaps it should be no surprise that the worse the writing, the more buzzwords abounded.

Frequent contributions also flowed in from others. The most prolific was psychologist and consultant Paul Thorne, whose profession is rife with non-words. Among others on whom I depended were Jonathan Kapstein, Leigh Bruce, Jules Arbose, Georgina Lack, David Manasian, Richard Evans, Sara Render, Michael Hyde, Mary Weed, Robert Neff, Paul Jenkinson, and for occasional help on the etymology, Anne Soukhanov. And for countless hours at the word processor, I am thankful to my daughter Raphaelle.

For his initial faith in this subject as book material, and his continuing support, I am grateful to Tim Goodfellow of Basil Blackwell, Oxford. For her keen eye in the editing process, I thank Halina Boniszewska, also of Basil Blackwell.

*   *   *

Publisher's Note:
All the cartoons in this book were drawn by the author.

INTRODUCTION

IT is a quirk of the mercantile society in which we live that no clear rules govern who may and may not rise to the ranks of business management. On one hand this has created a great meritocracy; on the other hand it opens business to anyone with a knack for making money or motivating others to do so. The result is a curiously mongrelized elite, a powerful class of people who come from other elite groups, such as law and accounting, as well as from the middle and lower reaches of society. Today throughout Europe, as in the United States, the business elite is emerging as the reigning elite.

One effect of this mixed population at the top of modern American and British business has been to make its language richer, more alive and in a sense wilder than that of any other profession. Lawyers have their jargon, but it is anchored in the Common Law writings of centuries ago. Medical doctors speak of body parts and processes in a weird *Latglish* hybrid memorized in medical school. English business jargon is different. Like a living organism, it grows and changes constantly.

But the evolution of business jargon is more than a mere academic curiosity. In some companies, those adept at using jargon are able to intimidate colleagues who have not kept up their vocabulary. A few years ago, Bendix Corp. in the United States was shaken by controversy when the young Harvard Business School graduate Mary Cunningham rose out of nowhere to become the chairman's powerful aide. One of her strengths was her masterly touch with the latest business school jargon. She literally talked her way to the top. Later, things got more complicated. The chairman ended up divorcing his wife and marrying her, and they were both thrown out of the company.

Business jargon flourishes best in the free-wheeling environment of the United States. The easy communication among managers of different levels encourages an easy language, unbound, irreverent and creative. Gradually, some of the Americanisms worm their way into the mother tongue. The description of growth industries as 'sunrise' industries (and the declining ones as 'sunset') can be spotted almost every week somewhere in the *Sunday Times*, but editor Andrew Neil says he picked it up during his travels in the United States. Most British readers today understand 'greenmail' because of the financial manipulations of Sir James Goldsmith, but the provenance is obviously American.

Today, anyone involved in international business is sure eventually to encounter an American whose speech is loaded with the latest jargon. Following a line of argument dressed up in such terms as 'bear hug' 'cash cow' and 'cleaning his clock' almost requires a translator. Yet many business executives are so much at home with their jargon that they are surprised to learn that it is not universal. Sometimes this attitude is simply naïve. An American negotiating in China recently lost contact with his opposite number entirely when, to emphasize the toughness of his company's position, he declared, 'In Pittsburgh, the bottom line is the bottom line is the bottom line.' His translator never figured out what he meant.

One of the main sources of business jargon today is the business schools that produce some 70,000 masters of business administration degree-holders (MBAs) every year in the United States, and some 3,500 in Europe. In the academic environment, business professors mix with their more pompous fellows in the philosophy department, inevitably acquiring some of the same stilt in their mode of expression. It simply wouldn't do to call something an 'example' if you can call it a 'paradigm'. And why say 'in comparison with' when *vis-à-vis* has such a learned ring? To be fair, the business school professors also bring to bear the tools of other disciplines – statistics, psychology, engineering – creating complex theories and solutions that require complex language to express them accurately.

A more dynamic source of new vocabulary is the men and women who actually run businesses. Every morning they face a range of challenges that few people outside the business world can appreciate. Often ridiculed by other professionals as philistine, one-dimensional and materialistic, on the average day business executives actually apply a wider spectrum of skills than most of their critics. To manage a large company in the dangerous world of global competition, the good executive knows something about mathematics, finance, psychology, international law, logistics, cross-cultural communications and manufacturing, to name a few. Many of these people are multilingual and widely travelled. Yet they spend most of their day in wood-panelled offices talking their way through their problems in the abstract, dealing at arm's length with some quite tangible matters. Doing an OVA, or overhead value analysis, is a very involved process on paper, but it can result in catastrophe for friends and colleagues if the numbers show that their jobs must go. It is this yearning to bring their pressures into focus, down to earth, that spawns such terms as 'downsizing', 'heavy hitter' and 'frag'. The real men among them also are nostalgic for sports and physical combat – that wellspring of so many of the metaphors they use in their daily jobs.

Lastly, the business writers themselves are guilty of playing with the language merely to enlighten an often shadowy subject. Thus the Fleet Street press in London stuck Swiss bankers with the colourful nickname 'gnomes of Zurich'. A correspondent for the US magazine *Business Week* invented 'conglomerosclerosis', and was bemused to see that it survived the magazine's multilayered editing process. You might say he 'threw it at the wall to see if it would stick', and it did.

Personally, I became interested in the jargon of business when I switched from political writing to business writing in the early 1970s. I was disturbed by the shorthand lingo that my editors considered good writing. Terms such as 'industry shakeout', 'jawboning' and 'critical mass' peppered the texts of my colleagues who were going places in the hierarchy. I quickly learned what was required of me, but I hope I never lost my ability to distinguish jargon from the English of general usage. When I became editor of *International Management*, a monthly business magazine for European executives, my sensitivity to jargon – and to Americanisms *vs* Anglicisms – was heightened. The magazine had to be comprehensible to executives reading us in English, usually their second language. Finally in 1987 I launched a monthly column entitled 'Business Buzzwords', from which about 20 per cent of this book is drawn.

This book is intended to enlighten the general reader in two respects: it explains the terms that business managers use in their daily lives, and through those terms it explains some of the trends at play in the business world today.

MICHAEL JOHNSON
London

A

Accountability

The doctrine of clear blame. Well-managed firms ensure that individuals are clearly identified with each risk undertaken. Success then is attributed to those who earned it, but failure is blamed squarely on those held *accountable*.

Acculturation

Getting accustomed to a new environment. Westerners in Japan start the process by learning to eat with chopsticks. Managers in a new corporate culture start the process by trying to understand what the chairman wants.

Acid test

Originally a test using aquafortis (nitric acid) to prove the presence of gold in a metal. Figuratively now applied to any crucial test – of a product, a strategy, an individual's performance.

ACORN

Market research acronym for A Classification Of Residential Neighbourhoods. ACORN helps marketers select target areas for specific products by analysing attitudes and buying power of neighbourhoods. The system, developed in the United States, is spreading to Europe. The US population has 44 ACORN types of neighbourhoods. Britain, slightly more homogeneous, has only 38.

Ad hocracy

The tendency to substitute ad hoc, or short-term, initiatives for serious, rational plans. Such behaviour works in an emergency, but when institutionalized it becomes a problem. Coined by futurologist Alvin Toffler, one of his many concepts that have become part of the language.

Adspend

Advertising industry shorthand for a company's annual budget for all kinds of advertising.

Advertorial

In publishing, the text that fills in around the advertising in special advertising sections of magazines and newspapers. So-called because the text is a hybrid of editorial and advertising copy. A dangerous amalgam because busy readers sometimes fail to distinguish the *advertorial* from the legitimate stories.

Affluenza

That nauseous, guilty feeling that creeps up on people who make more money than they think they are worth. Said to be rampant among MBA-holders and all stripes of YUPPIES. Sudden, windfall affluence is the cause, and influenza is what it feels like.

Aftermarket

The maintenance and spare parts business. Wise companies consider it a danger sign if the *aftermarket* is booming: it may mean a decline in quality and reliability of the product.

AIDA

Marketers' concept of the consumer's mental process of

Affluenza

deciding to buy. Step by step, the consumer moves from
Attention, to Interest, to Desire, to Action. Salesmen are alert
for signs that show their customer is on this slippery slope.

ALARA

In the nuclear power industry, the policy of controlling toxic
emissions (radioactive contamination) to the extent finan-
cially feasible. In the jargon of the industry, holding contamination 'As Low As Reasonably Achievable'. (See also
ALATA.)

ALATA

The ideal policy for those companies whose activities pose a
threat to the environment. It stands for maintaining contamination at levels 'As Low As Technically Achievable'. (See
also ALARA.)

Analysis paralysis

A common malady of timid managers: they are so cautious they often paralyse initiative by studying opportunities to death.

Arbitrageur

An investor who specializes in speculating on companies that may become take-over targets. The *'arbs'*, as such people are known, sell their holdings after take-over fever has sent the stock price through the roof. How the *arbs* find out who will be the next target of a PREDATOR is the mystery of the profession. Ivan Boesky did it the illegal way, by secretly acting on tips from investment bankers, and was jailed for INSIDER TRADING.

Armchair economics

Forecasting into virgin territory; any bold economic prediction based on insufficient data. A good example is the economic waffling over the impact of Europe's post-1992 Single Market; no region has tried such an ambitious integration of economic forces before, thus the results are necessarily reduced to mere guesswork.

Artificial intelligence

Computer systems that seek to imitate the thought processes of humans by recognizing language patterns and drawing inferences therefrom. Considered a computer application with great potential but as yet it is generally unrealized.

ASCII

American Standard Code for Information Interchange, a set of widely accepted technical standards for coding computer data intended for transmission over telephone lines.

Asset plays

Take-over of companies with property or other assets that are undervalued on the balance sheet. Some asset-heavy companies have an attractive BREAKUP VALUE because their real estate turned to gold while their operational earnings stagnated or deteriorated.

Asset redeployment

What new management often does to correct the alleged misjudgements of the previous team – sell this business, buy that business, and redeploy any excess cash in another. Sometimes it works, sometimes it is more like rearranging the furniture.

Asset-stripping

The selloff of company businesses to amass cash. Sometimes done to survive a period of poor performance; sometimes done by a new owner after an unfriendly take-over. The new owner sees business from a different perspective – its BREAKUP VALUE.

Atomistic

In product development, a way of studying a product's market potential by looking at the component parts of its overall impact. Borrowed from modern philosophy, where the ATOMISTIC approach holds that all propositions are made up of small, independent parts. The opposite of HOLISTIC.

Attrition

The reduction of payroll through the normal course of work-force mobility: resignations, retirements and death. In Britain, also known as *wastage*. Some companies plan payroll contraction by setting attrition targets. It was an accepted method of trimming staff until recently when trade union officials in Detroit awakened to the trend of shrinking membership. Now some US car makers have agreed to an anti-*attrition* clause, called SECURED EMPLOYMENT LEVELS. (See also SEL.)

B

Back office infrastructure

The systems and procedures of the unseen parts of a financial institution, such as the computerized processing of deposits and loans at retail banks. Front office is for customer contact. *Back office* is for planning what to do with the money after the customer leaves. Also known as 'Back end'.

Back to the future

A corporate strategy for the future that requires slimming down to core businesses, shedding activities perceived as distracting. Often the company ends up looking much as it did early in its history. Thus it reverts to the past in search of a more successful future.

Backward integration

A company's increasing involvement in earlier and earlier stages of the manufacturing chain. The paper maker that begins to produce pulp, then buys pine or eucalyptus forest land, is into *backward integration*. Sometimes a way of guaranteeing quality and supply; sometimes a trap locking you into inflexibility.

Bait and switch

A sales technique by which customers are lured into an establishment or a bidding process with a low-cost proposition. Once the customer has shown interest, however, it turns out that the 'bargain' has vanished (sold out, changed price, changed terms), and the seller offers a more costly substitute.

Basket case

A person, a company or an effort that has collapsed so hopelessly that it would have to be loaded into a basket to continue. Figuratively speaking, the Soviet economy is a *basket case*. So are many state-owned companies in Europe.

Bean-counter

The most primitive form of accountant: he or she who counts 'beans'. By extension, and in the unkindest spirit, managers' slang for all accountants when financial control seems too tight. In such conditions, blame for failure and problems is commonly attributed to the *bean-counters*.

Bear

A timid investor, or a retreating market, so-called because bears by nature keep their distance from humans – except when very hungry, when they *eat* humans.

Bear hug

The crushing embrace of your friendly partner through domination. The hug is nice at first, then it becomes restrictive.

Bells and whistles

Pejorative description of your competitor's alleged improvements on each new product. You want to believe he is only making minor changes, like the bells and whistles on a toy, to deceive the customer.

Bellwether industries

Those sectors, such as chemicals and steel, whose performance serves as a leading indicator of the direction the economy might take in the coming month, quarter or year. Originally, a wether was a sheep, and the *bellwether* was the head sheep that wore the bell. Thus if the shepherd could hear the bell, he could determine which way the flock was moving.

Belly-up

The posture of a bankrupt company or individual, *belly-up* like a dead fish floating in water.

Big bang

The pretentious nickname attached to the modernization and deregulation of London's financial markets in 1986. Borrowed from the theory of the same name describing the creation of the universe. Almost exactly a year later, the *bang* had turned to a whimper as the London Stock Exchange, like the New York Stock Exchange, plunged after Black Monday.

Big eight

For many years the world's leading auditing/accounting/ management consulting firms: Price Waterhouse, Deloitte Haskins Sells, Ernst and Whinney, Arthur Andersen, Touche Ross, KPMG (formerly Peat Marwick and Mitchell), Coopers and Lybrand and Arthur Young. Now out of date because of a series of mergers.

Big six

The producers of cars for Europe's mass market: Fiat, Volkswagen, Renault, Peugeot, Ford and Opel (General Motors).

Big ticket

Expensive, TOP-OF-THE-LINE. The *big ticket* computer is the big mainframe of IBM. The *big ticket* car is the fully equipped Mercedes.

Binary thinker

Another gem inspired by computer technology, this describes the person who tends to think in absolute terms – yes and no, black and white, good and bad – with no nuances in between. The binary feature of the computer is its capacity to answer all commands with a series of on–off, 0–1 type choices that eventually formulate a reply. The binary feature of the thinker is the ability to avoid grey areas. Everything in life becomes a yes-or-no proposition.

Bite the bullet

This is what tough guys do when the pressure is on. Originally, gunfighters in the Wild West found some relief from the pain of table-top surgery by biting a bullet as the amputation saw did its work. Now, very tough businessmen figuratively *bite bullets* when their profits are being amputated by competitors. In the most general sense, *bullet biters* are those who don't show their anguish when they encounter the less pleasant aspects of running a business. They just soldier bravely on.

Black box

In high-tech equipment, the unit that contains the proprietary technology, so secret that even REVERSE ENGINEERING cannot crack it. Also an aeronautics term for the crash-proof flight recorder, usually painted Day-Glo orange, however.

Bite the bullet

Black economy

The untaxed, undeclared work that cheats governments of their cut of workers' earnings or circumvents other inconvenient government regulations such as safety or environmental controls. The 'justification' is that government regulation or taxation is excessively onerous.

Black ships

Japanese slang for foreign invaders in the business world. The original *black ships* were Commodore Perry's, the US Navy officer who in 1853 used 'gunboat diplomacy' to force Japan to open its ports to free trade.

Blink rate

In advertising research, the number of times a reader blinks while reading an advertisement. The more blinks, the less concentration, and the less effect.

Blip

A transitory problem in a business that causes a short-term change in results. (See also GLITCH, HICCUP.)

Blockbuster

In pharmaceuticals, drugs that are so successful they affect the creator-company's balance sheet significantly. Valium was a *blockbuster* drug for Hoffmann Laroche. Tagament did the same for Smith Kline.

Blow-in

Advertising cards machine-stuffed into magazines during the binding process, and usually dumped by readers who shake out the publication on the street, in the train, or occasionally over a rubbish bin.

Blue chip

As every poker player knows, the *blue chips* are the most valuable. In stock market activity, the *blue chips* are the big companies with a long TRACK RECORD of high performance. In short, the best investment for the investor who has a low tolerance for risk.

Blue sky

Dreamy ideas for the future that are unlikely ever to be feasible. In the securities industry, testing a new issue against the regulations of different markets.

Bodycount

In a massive employee cutback, the number of people to be laid off. The opposite of HEADCOUNT.

Body language

The small, revealing movements you or your opposite number might make — in negotiations, for example — telegraphing private thoughts and feelings. In cross-cultural negotiations, a key to staying in the game. Thus, a Japanese scratching his head does not indicate dandruff. It indicates he is annoyed or angry.

Body shop

Employment agency or executive search consultancy with no sense of discrimination. A client is presented with what appears to be a random list of candidates for a job, few of whom are appropriate. The common denominator of all candidates proposed for a position is often no more than the fact that they are all warm bodies, hence *body shop*.

Bottleneck

An attempt of the dismal science, economics, to give colour to the concept of inadequate production capacity. The *bottleneck* makes it impossible for supply to meet demand, one of the basic causes of inflation. French economists use a plumbing term: *goulot d'étranglement*, the narrowing of a pipe that can cause the blockage of fluid. The results in either case can be extremely messy.

Bottom fishing

Seeking out cheap, poor-performing stocks that might rebound in price.

Bottom-heavy

An organization with a bulge in its lower ranks. Sometimes the PIG IN A PYTHON can be the cause of the disproportionate swelling. The opposite of top-heavy, and just as dangerous to survival.

Bottom line

The only line in a balance sheet that matters to some companies – the profit figure. While a common expression in the United States and Britain, not a household term elsewhere. An American from Pittsburgh recently caused confusion in China when, insisting on a better deal, he told his opposite number, 'The bottom line is the bottom line is the bottom line.' His translator rendered this as 'The line is on the bottom, always on the bottom, never on the top.'

Bottom out

When a performance curve finally reaches the low point and prepares to rise again. The opposite of TOP OUT.

Boutique

A subdivision of an integrated set of businesses or services. *Boutiques* specialize. They do one thing very well.

Bracket creep

In countries where higher incomes are taxed at higher rates, creeping up this scale of rates becomes a problem, especially in inflationary times. With each surge of prices and incomes, the tax bite increases faster than purchasing power, resulting in a net loss. US tax reforms of 1986 addressed the problem by creating fewer tax brackets with wider spacings.

Brain candy

Any mental activity that is both soothing and passive, like bad television or trashy fiction. In business, a warm syrup of platitudes that you give to your subordinates to make them feel comfortable, however briefly, about your latest mistakes.

Brainiac

The entrepreneur who is at once brilliant and mad. Every company should have one or two. Such people are frequently worth the trouble they engender, for the alternative is a team of conformists whose very caution limits its horizons.

Brainstorming

Spontaneous proposal of ideas, regardless of their practicality, in a group setting. A proven way to spark creative thinking through the removal of inhibitions.

Braintyping

Advertising research into tendencies of different groups that have RIGHT-BRAIN bias (emotional), or LEFT-BRAIN bias (logical). Once determined, the design and content of the advertising can be calculated accordingly. (See also LEFT BRAIN, RIGHT BRAIN.)

Breakup value

In *predators'* language, the unthinkable: what your company would be worth if greedy, heartless scoundrels bought it, then sold off its businesses one by one without regard for the sentiment and tradition that make it such a warm and homey place for you.

Bug, debug

A piece of equipment, software or any system that has minor

defects may be said to contain 'bugs'. Perhaps originally, sensitive machinery could be disturbed if live insects jumped or fell into the workings. In Welsh, *bwg* is a goblin. Today the term is used to describe a system's recurrent weakness. Frequently used in the computer software business during the painstaking process of development and testing. To eliminate the weakness is to *debug* it.

Bug

Bull

As a description of investors or market trends, it means aggressive, expansive. *Bulls* tend to charge.

Buppie

Black Urban Professional. (See also DINKY, PUPPIE and YUPPIE.)

Burnout

Psychological collapse after a long period of intense work. A common affliction of executives on the career ladder. Research in the 1970s established early signs of *burnout* such as behaviour changes, irritability, paranoia and exhaustion.

Business-as-usual budgeting

A set of numbers for next year built up with a fixed multiplier on top of this year's numbers. The multiplier is usually the established inflation rate. The danger is that errors can become built in over time. Such budgeting is unimaginative unless accompanied by a system for incorporating investment in legitimate areas. (See also ZERO-BASE BUDGETING.)

Buyback

A purchase on the open market of a company's own stock, thereby reducing the number of outstanding shares. A common defensive move against PREDATORS. The ploy raises the company's earnings per share, because the number of shares is reduced.

Buzzwords

In the business world, terms that capture the big trends and issues of the moment. The terms sometimes survive only as long as the trends. *Buzzwords* of the recent past include such terms as 'flexitime' and 'codetermination', now rarely heard.

C

CAD/CAM

Computer-Aided Design and Manufacturing, a technology spreading rapidly in WORLD CLASS industrial companies.

Camembert

See PIE CHART.

Can-do

An attitude of individuals or companies that love a challenge. 'We're a *can-do* kind of company.'

Captive market

The seller's dream: a group or customers who need a product, and have no choice but to buy yours, at whatever price you set. Some computer makers have tried this, with much success. In the end, however, the market rebels, for as nature abhors a vacuum, the market abhors captivity. Eventually, competitors will find a way in.

Career gridlock

Congestion at the top of the pyramid. *Gridlock* has hit your company when the pace of advancement seems to slow down for everyone at the same time. What has happened is probably the result of two converging trends: reduction of management positions as part of cost-control efforts, plus the arrival at promotable age of too many eligible 'baby boom' adults ready for advancement. If *career gridlock* has hit your company, it may be time to move on.

Career-limiter

An ill-considered, ill-timed statement or initiative by an ambitious junior executive – something so shocking to his superiors that his further advancement is compromised. Layers above him in the pyramid look askance, and mentally 'sidetrack' his career. ('This person is not one of us.') In proud and independent companies, suggesting a merger with the competition might be a *career-limiter*. In TOP-DOWN companies, overzealous criticism of the chairman's favourite themes might do it.

Cash cow

A product or a business in a company that generates revenue without further investment. Like a cow giving milk, the product or business is a reliable money maker. Yet *cash cows*, like milk cows, do require a certain minimum amount of tending. More importantly, owners should remember that cows of all kinds have finite lifespans.

Cashless society

The dream conjured up by credit card companies – the day when all purchases will be made with PLASTIC, and the card companies will rake off a percentage of each expenditure. Retailers' resistance to the stiff commissions charged by some cards makes their acceptance uneven, however, lessening the chances of the *cashless society* ever becoming a reality.

Casino society

The emergence of more and more ways to make money without actually performing productive work. It used to be called gambling.

Catchup

Some companies can never seem to achieve first place and are doomed to play *catchup* as they try to equal No. 1.

Champion

The executive or ranking manager who adopts a product development plan as his personal mission, and shepherds it through corporate resistance for funding and priority. Without a *champion*, a project is vulnerable to the company's multiple quantitative screens.

Change agent

An element of company strategy that serves as a catalyst to speed up a process of change. The *change agent* can be a person, an acquisition or a new policy at the top. Companies attempting to break out of old, uncompetitive patterns seek out a dramatic *change agent* to signal to employees that a new order has arrived.

Charisma

An essential quality of leadership, especially the ability to inspire employees through the spoken word, that sets outstanding leaders apart from others. A debate rages over whether *charisma* can be learned or must be inborn.

Chemistry

The affinity that develops among like-minded persons or complementary types in a well-chosen team. Good *chemistry* among co-workers at any level can spark *synergy*, and make $2 + 2 = 5$. Bad *chemistry* can wreck the best-laid plans.

Chickenfeed

Small sums of money. Often used ironically, as when applied

to the multimillion-dollar fines imposed on Wall Street offenders to whom such staggering penalties are insignificant, viewed from their comfortable financial perspective.

Chinese wall

The imaginary wall that is supposed to separate departments in financial institutions and thus prevent them from trading information in illegal ways. Named after the Great Wall of China, but too often breached, with criminal results, in recent times. (See also FIRE WALLS.)

Chips

The fingernail-sized flakes of silicon etched microscopically to contain tiny electric circuits for almost anything powered today by mains current or batteries – computers, hair dryers, car ignition systems, electronic drums for rock bands. *Chips* contain integrated circuits (ICs), probably the most important technological leap of the age, permitting the miniaturization of thousands of products.

Churning

A money-making but unethical practice of stockbrokers who are paid on the basis of each change in an investor's portfolio. The guidelines are vague, so it is up to the investor to resist the broker's enticements to try something new.

Circuit breaker

One of the controversial new ideas being discussed for stock exchanges to help prevent the herd instinct from causing market collapses of the variety experienced in October, 1987. The *circuit breaker* would kick into action and halt trading as prices of certain stocks swing beyond fixed bands. The mechanism would work much like an electrical circuit breaker, which interrupts surges of current to protect the system from melting down.

Cleaning his clock

A thorough, irreversible, uncompromising victory over an adversary. Of unknown origin, the phrase seems to evoke the total dismantling of the opposition into hundreds of tiny pieces, like the components of a clock, leaving the *cleaner of the clock* in supreme control of the victim's destiny. US author Thomas Peters said in an interview in 1988 that he believed many European companies were about to have their '*clocks cleaned*' by more astute international competitors. A fearsome prospect.

Clone

Borrowed from the world of biotechnology, where it means replicating cell structures, *clone* has been adopted by marketeers to designate products that duplicate offerings already available. Widely used in the computer industry, where *cloning* also implies doing it cheaper. IBM *clones*, for example, are machines that claim similar performance but sell at one-fifth the price. Not an illegal practice if done carefully.

Closed pitch

The consultant's dream. A presentation to a client who wants a *pro forma* explanation of your services but has already made up his mind to do business with you. *Closed pitches* are often organized for the benefit of the client's superiors who sit in to watch, but don't ask hard questions.

Closed probe

A question in market research that elicits a limited response, usually a 'yes' or 'no' answer. The ultimate in *closed probes* might be the aggressive American expression 'Am I right or am I right!'

Clutter effect

The declining impact of an advertisement due to crowding with other ads. Often a problem in print, radio and television.

Coaster

The executive who feels he or she has accomplished life's major goals, and can now afford to *coast*, or drift, through those last few years into retirement. This is a dangerous state of mind in companies that have adopted the lean management mode. *Coasters* often find themselves in retirement earlier than they had planned.

COLA

The extra compensation some expatriate executives are paid to help offset the inconvenience and lost property equity incurred by living away from home base. The *COLA* (Cost Of Living Allowance) is intended to bring them up to the standard of living they would be enjoying had they stayed at headquarters.

Cold call

A sales call to a prospect who has not indicated prior interest in the product being offered. Standard practice in door-to-door sales or telephone sales. Often a sign of desperation, though, when used by salespeople who normally work from lists of legitimate leads (it means they have run out of leads). Also a verb, as in this kind of boast: 'I *cold-called* him, and closed the sale in 10 minutes.'

Cold call

Comp and ben

A subdivision of the modern human resources department (mainly American) that specializes in compensation and benefits (known in Britain as remuneration and perquisites) policies and strategies. These are the people who advise management on ways to squeeze your pension payout, offload your dental plan or delay next year's salary increase.

Company doctor

A rare speciality in business: a person who enjoys taking on problem-companies and sorting them out, then moving on to another problem-company. Such people are not looking for roots; they thrive on the challenge of turning companies from loss to profit.

Computer nerd

A technically orientated person for whom the computer is God. In such people, all energies and emotion are channelled into matters related to hardware and software. Marketeers have identified them as a segment worth pandering to. Companies with ageing groups of *computer nerds* on the payroll find them difficult to promote or reward because of their narrow outlook and their generally poor human skills. A type of TECHNOID, *Nerd* is a form of *nert*, which in turn is a corruption of *nut*.

Computer shy

A temporary disorder of modern life in which a person imagines himself incapable of mastering even USER-FRIENDLY computer software. With each new generation, the incidence of this condition is diminished through education and the increasing appeal of benefits of computer culture. In France, *computer-shyness* is being stamped out by the free distribution of Minitel terminals by the postal and telecommunications authorities.

Concert party

In private investment circles, a group that conspires to acquire the same stock, and votes as a bloc to influence the price or the company. Illegal in some countries.

Consumer dissonance

An uneasy feeling of doubt experienced by customers after making a purchase.

Contrarian

In finance, the investor who systematically goes against the broad trends of the market. The theory is that a flood of interest in an issue means it is probably overpriced. *Contrarians* with staying power are often proven right.

Conventional wisdom

Coined by Canadian-born economist John Kenneth Galbraith, this term describes the accepted version of events — the version that probably needs to be challenged. Also known as RECEIVED WISDOM.

Cookie-cutter branch

Retail banking lingo for bank branches that look pretty much identical, regardless of the neighbourhood in which they are located. A recent, more popular, school of thought says branch design should be tailored to fit in with local architecture and design. The customer is thus lulled into a sense of being in friendly, familiar surroundings.

Core business

What is left after stripping away all the diversifications that were supposed to protect you from the cyclical effects of your original product speciality. Some of the conglomerates of the 1960s returned to their *core businesses* in the 1980s. Others, like ITT, dropped their *core business* and plunged into their diversifications.

Corporate ecosystem

The total environment in which a company operates, encompassing the 'ecology' of all organisms with which it interacts — government regulation, consumers, competition, labour unions.

Corporate saboteur

Surprisingly, a complimentary term for the suddenly popular maverick executive – the man or woman who wants to dispense with tradition and redirect the company along lines that make more objective sense. These people are either loved or hated, sometimes both, by colleagues who live within the bounds of a company's traditional ways.

Corporocracy

In countries where business culture is riding high, the self-styled elite class that runs industry. Business achievements confer upon the *corporocrats* an aura of distinction akin to the aristocracy of old. Does not apply in Britain, where the place of the industrialists is still uncertain.

Cosmeceuticals

Pronounced koz-muh-SUE-ticals, this is the new term for pharmaceuticals that have primarily a cosmetic effect, such as dewrinkling cream that disguises the ageing process of human skin. Drug companies are focusing on *cosmeceuticals* as a new growth area for the 1990s.

Couch potato

Market research lingo to designate lethargic television addicts. Such people eat too much junk food while stupefied by television programming. Eventually they acquire the physical profile of a large potato. Marketing executives speak in terms of 'surveying the *couch potatoes*' to determine viewer trends.

Critical mass

A term borrowed from nuclear physics – the mass needed to

cause a chain reaction. In business, dominant market share, or, by extension, the size needed to survive against international competition.

Crunch

The moment at which economic reality can no longer be ignored. One of many examples of violent metaphor enlivening an abstract business concept. Nothing actually goes 'crunch' except perhaps the careers of those unprepared when the *crunch* comes.

CSF

The elements that make the difference between success and failure in a company's operations. Although an annoying example of business-school jargon, the *CSFs*, or *Critical Success Factors* are useful to identify. Once determined, they help focus the mind on the important aspects of the business.

Customer-driven

An attitude of management that places the customer's wishes first. Any consumer product company probably recognizes the customer's pre-eminence. Other businesses are gradually coming round.

Cutting edge

In our tireless forward movement through time and space, hard-driving executives instinctively want to be in the lead – on the edge that cuts into new dimensions. High-tech companies are especially preoccupied with their *cutting-edge* credentials. There are lots of other edges on which one can survive in business, but it's the cutters who show the way. The trick is to stay there for more then one product cycle.

Cyclicality

One of the banes of the business world, and therefore fertile ground for theorizing. Some economists believe in growth–recession cycles of specific, predictable lengths. Large companies try to mix their businesses to include a balance of counter-cyclical activities to offset the inevitable downturns.

Cypherphobe

See COMPUTER-SHY.

D

Daisy chain

In finance, a surreptitious linkage of buyers who concentrate on one stock or group of stocks with the intent of driving the price up. The *chain* is then broken, leaving the innocent investor with overpriced holdings. Illegal in most countries. (See also CONCERT PARTY, WASH-TRADE.)

Daisy wheel

A technology for computer printers that produces high-quality (so-called LETTER-QUALITY) print on paper. The term comes from the shape of the plastic disk containing letters and numbers on the tips of the wheel's 'petals'. With some imagination, the wheel might be said to resemble a daisy. Unfortunately the 'petals' break off almost as easily as they do on the real thing.

D&B

Executive suite shorthand for 'Different and Better', the criteria all companies seek in order to distinguish their products from the competition's wares. If a product is short on originality, smart managers get to work on finding ways to boost the *D&B* quotient.

Danegeld

Originally a British tax paid to the Danes in the tenth and eleventh centuries to stop rape and pillage by the stronger Danes. Now in business, any form of blackmail. By extension, the assessment imposed on a subsidiary by a multinational to help pay for headquarters' services and overheads. Often seen by the subsidiaries as an excessive burden, hence the association with *Danegeld*.

Databation

Not as rude an activity as might be assumed, *databation* is the manipulation of computerized databases for the sheer pleasure of it. Computer buffs claim that their aimless wanderings through databases can lead to unexpected finds.

Data colouration

The little white lies that percolate up the line as employees at all levels report the state of their business in the most favourable light possible. A salesman who takes a risk by prematurely reporting a successful deal is *colouring data*. So is the accountant who slides this year's expenses into next year's budget. It is an art form when done well; a SACKABLE OFFENCE when not.

Dawn raid

A financial move by a PREDATOR company at the opening bell of stock market trading. Like many BUZZWORDS, this one comes from guerrilla warfare, in which the warriors hope to catch their opponents napping.

DDD sensation

A signal, in California terms, that your career may be headed in the wrong direction because it has become 'Difficult, Distasteful and Depressing'. (To solve your problem, see EEE.)

Death Valley curve

The stage in a new company's existence when losses erode its equity base, damaging its ability to raise new funds.

Rarely used outside venture capital circles, and even there only whimsically.

Deception by omission

A marketing and advertising technique used by companies of limited scruple. The idea is to avoid mentioning aspects of the product that might discourage the discriminating buyer. A food product might scream 'NO PRESERVATIVES' on a package, but still contain colouring, artificial flavouring, artificial sweetener and other questionable ingredients.

Decision Support System

A new family of software packages for executives who use desktop computer terminals. The *Decision Support System*, or *DSS*, provides easily accessed models of the situation facing the company. WHAT-IF games can help support the executive decision with better data and an indication of the impact that might result from a change of one or more factors.

Deep pockets

Large cash reserves, and a willingness to dip into them. In a close competitive struggle, it is important to know how deep your opponent's pockets are.

Deindustrialization

The shift in a national economy from industrial production into services such as banking, finance, insurance, information services and other intangibles. Worrisome if a strong trend because erosion of the industrial base means permanent loss of important capabilities and therefore dependence on others to supply them – at a price determined by them.

Delist

An option that many companies began to consider after the crash of October, 1987. Firms that lost more than a third of their net worth were tempted to *delist*, or retire from the fray by going private and withdrawing the company from the stock exchange listing. Private companies, those that are not 'listed', may find it harder to raise financing, but they are spared the roller coaster ride of share-value swings.

Demassify

A made-up verb invented to describe the process of reorganizing a company into smaller, more entrepreneurial units. The way of the future, it would seem, because people have more latitude for creativity and innovation in smaller business units.

Demerger

What occasionally ensues when the marriage or merger of two companies proves counterproductive or incompatible. They divorce, or *demerge*, and go their separate ways. All too often, partners caught in this trap suffer in silence, fearful of the complexity of *demerging*. As a result, the *demerger* rate is minuscule compared to the merger rate.

Differentiation

The development of products or services that are demonstrably different from those of the competition. *Differentiation* is sometimes a key marketing advantage in a crowded room of ME-TOO PRODUCTS.

DINKY

Now widely used in younger circles for dual-career couples.

It stands for 'Dual Income, No Kids Yet'. Like the YUPPIE, possibly a disappearing species.

Dinosaurs

Large companies managed in old-fashioned ways, too big and cumbersome to survive in today's world of global competition.

Discontinuities

The incidents in a company's development that require more than evolutionary adaptation. A technological *discontinuity* was the development of solid-state electronics to replace valves (vacuum tubes). Other market or product developments have been as disruptive: the advent of phototypesetting, the invention of synthetic fibres and the growth of air travel. Each of these posed a *discontinuity* problem for the traditional industry. Many failed to bridge the gap to the new technology.

Disintermediation

In financial deregulation, the removal of an intermediary (for example, the banks) from the chain of money-handlers separating the individual investor from the publicly traded shares he is buying. *Disintermediation* streamlines the process and reduces the consumer's fees, but costs the intermediary dearly.

Dividend-lopping

When times are hard, and investment eats all the cash, an easy option is to reduce payout to shareholders, or 'lop off' the dividend.

Dochakuka

For Japanese businessmen abroad, the technique of adapting to local conditions, sometimes called 'global localization'. The word is borrowed from Japanese agriculture, where it means adjusting your planting, fertilizing and harvesting methods to meet local soil conditions.

Dochakuka

Dog and pony show

Slang for any business presentation with show-business trappings, audio-visual equipment or multiple participants. Appropriately, borrowed from the circus.

Doing lunch

An action-oriented synonym for the more ordinary 'having

lunch'. 'Taking lunch' is also in vogue. The meaning is the same. Drinking lunch is for the desperate, and skipping lunch is for the overweight, or the very, very busy.

Done deal

An agreement, an assumption of an agreement, or a self-evident commitment between two parties. A *done deal* is an arrangement that engages both parties, but may have started as a casual handshake. 'Don't worry about the order I promised. It's a *done deal*,' your customer might tell you. He probably means it.

Dot matrix

A popular technology for inexpensive computer printers. Letters are punched out at lightning speed through the electronic control of pins striking a ribbon and paper. The cheaper the printer, however, the more difficult the dots are to decipher. (See also NLQ.)

Dotted-line relationships

On an organization chart, or ORGANOGRAM, the linkages between executives and the subordinates they oversee on a less than day-to-day operational basis. *Dotted-line* can sometimes mean whatever the person at the high end of the line wants it to mean. Your *dotted-line* superior may be watching, or he may be otherwise engaged. It is important to know.

Double-dipping

Getting double benefits from a tax or compensation system, often by illegal or dubious means. Dual-career couples abroad, both receiving full housing and COLA payments for their families, are *double-dipping*.

Download

Computerspeak for 'receive'. Used in the manuals of the soft-ware writers to signify receiving a communication from another computer. (See also UPLOAD.)

Downmarket

A step down the class ladder in the marketplace; a poor quality product; a kind of business your peers would think unworthy of you. (See also UPMARKET.)

Downsizing

Trimming waste by producing smaller products. Especially common in the car industry, where consumers sometimes revolt against the manufacturer's excesses. Daimler Benz satisfied this revolting group by adding a *downsized* model to its range, the Mercedes 190, in the early 1980s.

Downstream

Everything that happens in the production process after your company's activity. If you manufacture water taps, the sink assembly is *downstream* from you.

Downtime

The days, hours, or minutes your machinery sits idle await-ing maintenance or spare parts.

Drip-feeding

In venture capital, the practice of injecting cash in small incre-ments during a STARTUP's initial years. Cash is the lifeblood of a growing business, hence the natural attraction of this intra-venous metaphor.

Drive

A verb that has acquired a transitive meaning in the business world as action-orientated executives push and pull their way through the marketplace, as in driving a team of horses. An innovative computer company chairman might say things like: 'What *drives* this company? Technology.' A company focused on quarterly results might be BOTTOM-LINE driven. (See also CUSTOMER DRIVEN.)

Drop-dead graphics

Computer industry term for high-definition graphics, of a higher order than previously believed possible. In effect, graphics so startling to the user that he almost *drops dead* of surprise. Typical computer industry hyperbole.

E

Early adopters

In the marketing of pharmaceuticals through the medical profession, those doctors who readily agree to try out new medicines. By extension, the first wave of customers for any regulated product.

ECU

The European Currency Unit, an average value of several European currencies closely managed by their central banks. The intent is to calm the wild swings in exchange rates against the US dollar and other currencies.

EEE sensation

That California kind of feeling that tells you to proceed in the direction you are moving because it is 'Easy, Effortless and Enjoyable'. By following this beacon faithfully, you will end up discovering your true purpose in life. (For the opposite, see DDD SENSATION.)

Empty suits

The colourless, robot-like executives produced by long careers in TOP-DOWN corporations. In such companies, middle management can be as invisible and passive as *empty suits*.

Endaka

The punishment many Western businessmen think the Japanese have deserved for the past 15 years. *Endaka* means a high yen and all the competitive problems thereby entailed.

Empty suit

Enter

We used to say, 'Please type this.' Now, in the age of word processing, we say, 'Please *enter* this.' The computer industry has convinced us that we are no longer simply typing, we are *entering* data into the computer memory.

EPOS

Electronic systems that keep track of inventory levels on a real-time basis. The moment a purchase is registered, the *EPOS* (for Electronic Point Of Sale) system deducts the item from warehouse records. Some systems automatically trigger an order of new supplies when pre-programmed levels are reached.

Ergonomics

The study of man's integration with machine, especially in the design of products with a natural fit. *Ergonomics* today governs the shape of everything from cars to computers.

Ergonomically excellent products are those that save the user aches and pains. Detachable keyboards, adjustable steering wheels, orthopaedic office furniture all grew out of *ergonomics*. High-heeled shoes and chopsticks did not.

Europe, Inc.

The aim of the Single Market initiative in the European Community: the creation of a coordinated economic power including the combined industrial might of all 12 countries. Possibly some day a counterweight in the world economy to JAPAN, INC and the United States.

Excellence

Once a word simply meaning a high degree of merit, now a term with multiple reflections, reverberations and distortions prompted by the publishing phenomenon *In Search of Excellence* by Thomas Peters and Robert Waterman. In the mid-1980s, *excellence* became a rallying call in companies worldwide for a wide spectrum of objectives – sales, profit, productivity, quality, personal motivation, innovation. Even the Japanese picked it up. The business monthly *Nikkei Business* featured a list of *ekserentu kompani*.

Exdexing

The study of stock indexes to determine which securities are *not* on the high-profile lists. CONTRARIANS use this technique on the theory that indexed issues will attract too many buyers, automatically driving the price too high.

Exit interview

Standard practice of personnel departments when key employees resign – structured interviews are conducted to determine sources of dissatisfaction within the company.

Troublesome managers up in the hierarchy are sometimes identified in this way.

Export substitution

A protectionist move by a government attempting the impossible: to halt the flow of international goods into its territory. Locally produced goods are substituted for items that normally would be imported. The long-term result is to slow economic development by opting out of global competition and allowing local industry to enjoy a protected business environment.

Eyebrow management

An arm's-length management style by which a top executive can stop a course of action with the merest hint of disapproval – in effect by raising his or her eyebrows. Beware of this type of individual when aroused.

Eyebrow management

Eye contact

The annoying practice of feigning sincerity and intensity by staring into people's eyes while listening or talking. The uninitiated often think they are having an intimate experience, only to discover they have been stared down by mere *eye contact*.

F

Failing forward

In risk-taking companies, a learning process that consists of trying something − a product, a strategy, an organizational change − and scrapping it for a better idea if it doesn't work. Thus each failure leads to an improvement. At IBM, they have invented a close cousin, 'failed success'. This is the product that is right in every conceivable way, but never made it in the marketplace. A string of failed successes would be the act of *failing forward*.

Fairweather market-maker

A broker who trades in high volume for his own personal account in good times.

Fan club

In investment circles, a group of people coincidentally investing in the same stock but for different reasons. Contrary to the CONCERT PARTY, *fan clubs* are legal.

Fast lane

A very successful manager's career path. Also any business or a part thereof that turns over more money or grows much faster than average. The term, borrowed from the highway, is normally used in the large sense: 'At my company we live our lives in the *fast lane*.'

Fast track

The career path on which every new MBA hopes to ride to

the top, preferably by the age of 30. Reserved for outstanding performers or close relatives of top management.

Fax it

A phrase that entered the language suddenly in the late 1980s as facsimile machines sprouted like mushrooms in business offices, replacing inefficient postal services and more complex telex systems. The magic of the 'fax' hurt courier services most of all.

Feedback loop

A refinement system in which designated players continuously communicate their findings to each other so as to improve a solution. It is a management science concept that attempts to structure the search for a solution, then monitors it through implementation and back to the beginning again, as often as necessary to optimize the solution. (See also IN THE LOOP.)

Fibre snobs

In the garment trade, this is a deprecatory term for consumers who refuse to wear artificial fibres. The garment industry lives in fear of a backlash against polyester and its cousin. Discriminating consumers who can still afford natural fabric prefer it for its look, its touch and the fact that it is not a by-product of the petrochemical industry.

Finder's fee

A payment made to middlemen for finding business opportunities or partners for others. Common in the publishing industry and high-technology businesses. In mergers and acquisitions, these deal-makers can collect as much as 3 per cent of the price of the acquisition.

Find time

The seconds or minutes required for consumers to spot your product on the shelf among competing brands. The object of the manufacturer is to reduce the *find time* to a minimum.

Fingerspitzengefühl

That ability a few lucky entrepreneurs have – an accurate feel for a situation, perceived as if through the fingertips. A German word with no English equivalent.

Fire drill

A scolding by supervisors; a reminder to employees that company procedures must be followed. Usually held after a crisis.

Fire walls

Those invisible barriers in financial institutions that prevent people in conflicting parts of the firm trading information with each other – loan officers and mergers and acquisition people, for example. Also used in the auditing trade, where auditing business can conflict with management consulting. If the *fire walls* do not hold, the ensuing conflagration can be very destructive. A synonym is CHINESE WALL.

Flattening the pyramid

The old way to organize companies – copied from the military – was to place an army of toilers at the bottom of the organizational pyramid and stack increasingly small layers of managers on top of them. The chairman sat alone at the peak. Today, those at the bottom complain vocally of the weight they must carry. *Flattening the pyramid* eliminates some of the middle management layers and brings senior management in closer touch with the workforce. Some egalitarian companies have abandoned the top-to-bottom concept altogether, arranging their tables of organization sideways. The question then becomes, does the chairman sit on the right or the left?

Flattening the pyramid

Flavour of the month

The latest fad in products, management gimmicks, pet employees or any other aspect of your job that is subject to changing tastes. Lifted from the ice cream parlour, where it is the flavour currently being promoted.

Flight capital

Savings, investment funds and bags of gold that flee abroad when a country takes a turn that bodes ill for growth, such as the election of a Socialist government. Capital controls sometimes follow, but too late.

Flight to quality

What happens to stock market funds when times are uncertain. Investors flee from risky companies towards quality, BLUE-CHIP stocks, to wait for the more generalized growth trends of good times to return.

FMCG

An acronym commonly used in recruitment advertising for executives trained in Fast-Moving Consumer Goods. Gibberish to everyone else.

Focus group

A group of consumers assembled by a manufacturer or market research firm to discuss and judge the potential of a product or service. The *focus group* members are paid, but are encouraged to be candid.

Foodies

Consumers who spend more than average on gourmet foods, junk food products and other innovative concoctions of the food industry. *Foodies* will eat anything so long as it is new and trendy.

Footfall

In the retail trade, the measurement of pedestrian traffic in front of the shop. Stores that depend on a high rate of drop-in customers require high *footfall* numbers. Specialized consultancies provide such data for a large fee.

Footfall

Forts and eagles

Insider jargon in high technology firms for the opposite extremes in company culture. The *forts* are the entrenched, backward-looking, defensive giants of yesteryear who are hanging on today by cost-cutting and asset-stripping. The *eagles* are the high-tech high-flyers who are making new rules as they go along.

Frag

Military slang dating from the Vietnam War, *frag* is a verb shortened from 'fragmentation grenade', a particularly deadly weapon. To *frag* an adversary in business is to attack him with intent to cause serious harm.

Frontrunning

A stockbroker who trades on his own account before ringing up clients to recommend the same buy. An ethical tightrope that has a long drop for those who become too daring.

G

Gaijin

Everyone in the world except the Japanese. It means 'foreigner' in Japanese and is only slightly less pejorative than the Spanish *gringo*. When the Japanese want to refer to you in polite terms, you become a *gaikokujin*.

Gainsharing

Compensation plans that share the financial gains of productivity improvements among all levels of employees. Widely and successfully implemented in small and medium-sized US companies as an incentive for higher quality work.

Game theory

A method of evaluating different business strategies by using mathematics to represent degrees of uncertainty. By working out the mathematics, the player can minimize risk, maximize profit, or balance risk and reward. (See also MAXIMAX, MAXIMIN, MINIMAX and ZERO SUM.)

Gap analysis

The art of guessing where your plan might, at some point in the future, diverge from reality. The analysis consists of making contingency plans for bridging the gap with supportive strategy in the production or marketing of a product. A lot of trouble, but good insurance.

Gatekeeper

Any person or institution that screens or selects. A personnel department interviewer is a talent *gatekeeper*. The mass media serve as information *gatekeepers*.

Gattable

Protectionist trade restraints thought to be within the letter, if not the spirit, of the General Agreement on Trade and Tariffs (*GATT*), and therefore defensible. Thus the European Community, in blocking the importation of hormone-laden US meat products, considered the move a *gattable* initiative.

Generics

Products similar to the major brand names, but without the cost burden of expensive packaging or advertising built into their price. Some supermarkets offer a wide range of *generics* under their own label, usually cheaper than brand names. In pharmaceuticals, the cheaper *generic* medicines move on to the chemists' shelves the day after patent protection expires. This often ends a period of easy cash for the brand holder.

Geodemographics

Market research term for analysis that combines geographical data with demographics, as in the ACORN system. The theory is that people with similar means and attitudes will live in the same neighbourhoods. A useful tool for direct-mail marketers. Anathema to those who dislike junk mail.

Geromarket

In demographics, the customers in the high age bracket. This is a growing market but is complicated by a decline in purchasing power due to the generally modest level of retirement income.

Ghosts

The masters of the art of milking the black economy by being economically productive while remaining outside the tax system. This is a term used by tax fraud squads whose job it is to find the *ghosts* and bring them to justice. Inevitably the fraud squads are called 'Ghostbusters'.

Givebacks

Concessions from trade unions or employees to ease financial strain on the company. A useful strategy if not abused. It backfired on General Motors, however, when blue-collar workers agreed to *givebacks*, then, the following year, saw top management awarded lucrative compensation terms for improvement in performance.

Glasnost

A Russian word enjoying vogue thanks to Mikhail Gorbachev and his innovative economic advisers in the Kremlin. Although the word is defined in Russian dictionaries as 'publicity', current usage has supercharged it to convey a sense of open discussion and debate of issues that previously would have been taboo in public Soviet forums.

Glass ceiling

The invisible barrier that blocks career progress. Women have been colliding with this ceiling for years. More and more, internationalists working for companies of foreign nationality are hitting it. A few are beginning to break through.

Glitch

A HICCUP, a BLIP, a temporary shortfall in performance or other pressing problem relatively easily corrected.

Glocal

The view of your marketplace simultaneously in global and local terms (global plus local). As usual, the Japanese do it best. They call it DOCHAKUKA.

Glowboy

A semi-skilled worker specializing in the rapid cleanup of nuclear contamination. The trick is to get in and out of the contaminated area before absorbing a lethal dose of radiation. *Glowboys* are adept at working very close to the limit. When they overstep the boundaries of safety, they 'glow' with the overdose.

Gnomes

Derisory term for bankers and money managers in Switzerland. Usually applied to '*gnomes* of Zurich'. The association seems to be the image of Swiss bankers as small, cruel, wizened creatures who originated as *gnomes* from the Alps. Actually, many of them are not that bad.

Going south

What the profit line on your performance chart starts doing when the going gets tough. Arch consultantspeak; not to be used by or with ordinary people.

Golden bullet

Originally a term from the pharmaceutical industry to designate a drug or medicine that focuses precisely on a disorder and eliminates it cleanly. Latterly, marketing-speak for that miracle product that shoots through the haze of competition and reaches the customer efficiently.

Golden handcuffs

The compensation package so attractive that it dissuades you from leaving a job you otherwise could not endure. Much like being in handcuffs, but nicer.

Golden hello

A substantial bonus payment to a valuable new employee recruited from outside. The extra cost of the 'hello' is a gamble considered safe because the new employee brings much-needed expertise to the hiring firm.

Golden parachute

A termination clause in a manager's contract that guarantees him or her a 'soft landing' no matter how poorly he has done his job. In the United States, these *parachutes* run into millions of dollars. Increasingly criticized, however, as the competitiveness of US companies sags.

Golden share

The one specially defined share in a company whose holder can block certain decisions. The *golden shareholder*, usually a government in a partially privatized company, can stop a strategy it disagrees with.

Goodness of fit

The degree of conformity between a theoretical model in market research and the actual data after analysis.

Gorbasm

The phenomenon of Gorbachev-worship at its worst. Coined by a disillusioned hard-line member of the Reagan administration, who defines it as a brief feeling of euphoria followed by a sense of disappointment.

Golden parachute

Go with the flow

Moving with the majority, making no waves, bending like a reed in the wind. *Going with the flow* is a safe but dull way to spend your professional career. Innovative companies profess to be looking for people who resist the flow, who make waves, who lean into the wind. Don't be too sure.

Grazers

People who don't eat, but graze, like goats, among snacks and foods. In some cases, confirmed *grazers* never actually have sit-down, organized family-style meals. A boon for the junk food business.

Greater fool

The theory that in a rising stock market it is safe to overpay for a stock because there is always a *greater fool* standing by who will come in at an even higher price.

Greenfield site

A virgin location outside an urban area for a plant or office building. The construction does not displace other buildings; it usually eats up farmland.

Gross up

In market research, extrapolation of a population sample to represent the entire population. In employee compensation, to *gross up* is to increase a payment such as a bonus or an award so that the net after-tax amount equals the original promised sum. Thus an employee winning a bonus of $10,000, but liable to a 25 per cent withholding tax, is actually paid enough so that he still has $10,000 to take home.

Groupthink

Irving Janis coined this word to characterize blind acceptance of the group's point of view against all contrary objective evidence. *Groupthink* is a hazard of current 'consensus management' and 'teamwork' concepts.

Grow

A relatively recent transitive usage borrowed from the

farmers and gardeners. Formerly, an executive might have said, 'Under my direction, this company will grow as never before.' Today, to give the statement a more aggressive, take-charge ring, the executive will say, 'I am going to *grow* this company.' It leaves no doubt who is sowing, and who intends to reap.

Guru

Originally a Hindu name for a spiritual teacher, or leader of a religious sect. In the 1960s, American original thinkers acquired the title as a semi-jocular nickname. By the 1980s, *guru* had entered the English language as a more serious honorary title for such authors and consultants as Edward de Bono and Peter Drucker. Most frequently used as 'Management *guru*'.

H

Hack

A worker without distinction. In Britain, mock self-deprecatory term for journalist (short for *hack* writer). Also appropriate for other professions, as in *hack* flute-player.

Halo effect

The spillover goodwill that strong performance in one narrow area can have on the same individual's performance in another. Thus an outstanding salesman, whose success this year saved the company, might be promoted next year to marketing vice president, his first management role, due entirely to the *halo effect* of his sales record. In cases where such promotions are unsuccessful, the company suffers from HALO ERROR.

Halo error

See HALO EFFECT.

Handout

Money advanced without obligation to repay. Research subsidies from government sources are the best kind to go for. Also, in public relations, slang for press release. In the conference business, the printed material distributed to back up a presentation.

Hands-on manager

This person can be a blessing or a curse, depending on how much his skills actually contribute to the productive effort.

He is *hands-on* because he descends from the executive suite to get physically involved with the business at all levels. An interesting variation was the chief executive of one European conglomerate who described himself as 'hands-off, but eyes-on'. His speciality was spotting the weaknesses in financial reports from the company's far-flung subsidiaries.

Hardball

Aggressive competition, no holds barred. *Hardball* is a faster, tougher version of softball. Commonly used in companies run by former or frustrated sportsmen.

Hardship pay

Extra compensation for expatriates working in difficult or dangerous conditions. Oilmen in Alaska, construction workers in the Middle East, soldiers in Greenland all receive substantial *hardship pay* on top of their salaries.

Hawthorne effect

The distortion of data when a test group knows what is expected of it. The original *Hawthorne effect* dates back to the 1920s at Western Electric in Hawthorne, Illinois, when managers decided to improve the work environment in order to make workers happier, therefore possibly more productive. The walls were repainted, and productivity improved. Shortly thereafter, the walls were repainted again. Productivity improved again. Soon the experimenters realized the workers were stepping up productivity not because they were happier but because they knew what was expected.

Headcount

The number of employees on the payroll.

Headhunter

This slang term for 'executive search consultant' has an interesting history in Europe. The British imported it from the United States, the French translated it literally into *chasseur de têtes*, the Germans use it in English (rejecting *Kopfjäger* as too savage), and the Italians have it both ways: sometimes as *cacciatore di teste* and sometimes in English.

Heavy half

In any population sample, the half in which the evidence you are looking for is concentrated. In a market survey, researchers might consider the wealthier 50 per cent of the sample to be the *heavy half*. (See also PARETO PRINCIPLE.)

Heavy hitters

In companies given to sports metaphor, the top performers. Also influential people such as financiers outside the company. *Heavy hitters* were originally baseball stars who hit the long ball.

Heroes, myths and legends

The story of where your company came from, who mattered, what victories made it what it is today. This is jargon of management development and training professionals who enjoy asking managers to identify their *HM and Ls* as a way of getting inside their minds, understanding the company's cultural imperatives.

Heuristic

A trendy substitute for 'unstructured' procedures. The word originates in education, where it applies to students who are allowed to search for knowledge without the conventional spoon-feeding from teachers; in computer science, problem-solving on a trial-and-error basis. Never try to run a company *heuristically*.

Hiccup

A temporary interruption in growth and development, due to a transitory problem. A one-quarter dip in profit might be a *hiccup*. A one-year dip is probably more serious. (See also BLIP, GLITCH.)

Hidden agenda

The true motives behind the behaviour of the person you are having trouble with. He/she might be your boss, your employee, your opposite number in negotiations, your spouse. For example, your subordinate's official agenda says he is discussing the need for 10 more staff, but his *hidden agenda* is his quest for a vice presidency. Guessing what is on this *hidden agenda* − what the meeting is *really* about − will speed the solution on its way. Usually the person with the secret agenda hides it carefully.

High-flyer

A young, upwardly mobile executive, often equipped with an MBA certificate, on his or her way to management heaven. The high-flyers are so named for their ability to bridge hierarchical barriers from an early stage, as if on wings. The lucky high-flyers eventually perch somewhere near the top of the pyramid.

High-net-worth

Portfolio managers' term for the very rich. Portfolio managers are paid a percentage of the sum they manage, thus the *higher the net worth* of the client, the better potential for large commissions.

Hip-shooter

An executive who operates from visceral impulses rather than deliberation. Such people often rate high on decisiveness, but need luck to hit targets consistently. The term comes from Hollywood cowboys who never bother to take careful aim.

Hired guns

In a take-over battle, the lawyers, accountants and other advisers brought in on retainers to help plan or execute strategy. A lucrative speciality in the United States, now emerging in Europe as industrial rationalization picks up momentum.

Hit squad

A term borrowed from organized crime, the *hit squad* is your acquisition team. In private, the team decides which companies to go after, then gathers the proper 'weapons', financial, psychological or otherwise, and sets about attacking the prey.

Hockey stick

A performance curve that descends sharply to a certain point, then rises just as sharply in a straight line. Typical of new products or start-up companies in the early stages. The shape vaguely resembles the bend in a hockey stick.

Holdbacks

In bargaining for technology-exchange agreements with

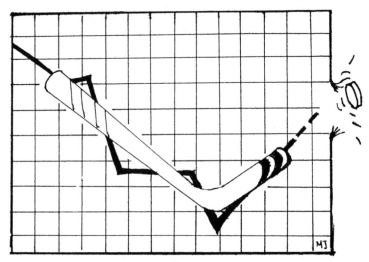

Hockey stick

other companies, *holdbacks* are the knowledge and techniques you exclude from the sharing deal, explicitly or secretly. In cases of secrecy, your partner will assume that you have *holdbacks*, but will often not make an issue of it because he has some of his own.

Holistic

An approach to management that encompasses the entire range of human needs, not just money. Also used in alternative medicine circles. A *holistic* manager really cares about your children, your hobby and the level of happiness you achieve in your work. The word comes from the jargon of philosophical discourse, where it means the careful ordering of things to produce a whole that is greater than the sum of its parts.

Hollow corporation

A company that subcontracts, or OUTSOURCES, most of its

manufacturing. The advantage is simplification and flexibility. The drawback is the loss of 'soul', the loss of control, the loss of identity.

Hot button

In marketing circles, the thing you push in order to get a strong response. You find this button by knowing what the market wants. You push it by becoming the first to supply it. Finding the market's *hot button* brings great rewards, but usually short-term only. The *hot button* has a bad habit of cooling off and moving to a new position. The best marketeers know how to find it quickly.

Housecleaning

In a reorganization, the dismissal of several managers at one stroke. If turnaround is the aim, a good *housecleaning* is often necessary, for management must bear the responsibility.

Humanoid

A sterile, unnatural personality type often found among senior managers. The *humanoid* spends his professional life keeping out of trouble, the result being a successful career but a broken spirit. Do not make jokes with such individuals.

Hunch marketing

Marketing conceived without detailed knowledge of, or research into, consumer needs. A strategy based on a feeling or a 'sixth sense' that makes it seem right. A good method for those with FINGERSPITZENGEFÜHL.

Hushmail

A financial incentive or payoff to a departing employee to guarantee his or her silence on certain sensitive company matters. A derivation of 'greenmail', which in turn derives from 'blackmail'.

Hushmail

I

Idiot-proof

Products that even the most inept consumer could not fail to operate correctly. The one-button point-and-click camera is an example. The software industry has a long way to go in this realm. (See also POKA-YOKE.)

Incentivize

Another in the US lexicon of verbs that grew out of nouns. To *incentivize* a management team is to give it something extra for superior performance, such as more money. Linguistically, in the same grey area as PRIORITIZE.

Industry shakeout

Darwin called it 'survival of the fittest'. In business, it is the crowding out of inefficient players in a maturing market following a period of expansion. Personal computer manufacturers have recently gone through a SHAKEOUT, leaving a few healthy survivors and dozens of wrecked companies.

Inertia selling

The dubious practice of invoicing customers for each new version of your product (usually once a year) even if unwanted, in the hope that the product will be accepted and the invoice paid. Especially prevalent in the business of expensive directories and other annual reference book revisions.

Information glut

The problem you face when you have gathered more in-

formation than you can digest. Telecommunications technology and computer systems have aggravated this problem in
the United States to such a degree that businesses sometimes
drown in data that should be keeping them afloat. The
winners in the rapidly expanding information business will
be those who help customers gain quick access to the
numbers and insights they actually need.

Information glut

Infotainment

Wallowing in the same linguistic sewer as COSMECEUTICALS,
this combination of 'information' and 'entertainment' describes the blending of showbusiness techniques with the
presentation of information, especially in television. 'Happy
talk' news presenters, now showing up in European markets,
are guilty of first-degree *infotainment* crimes.

In play

A company finds itself in play when buyers – friendly or hostile — are talking openly about acquiring a significant stake. Executives normally fear being 'in play' because a take-over may be imminent. Strategy thus falls apart, people leave, and the main topic on employees' minds becomes the take-over, not the competition.

Input

Contribution; a piece of a larger effort. Now becoming a trendy verb: 'I *inputted* heavily to that project.' Never say this.

Inside baseball

Knowledge of the finest nuances of a situation, and the display thereof. Sometimes an effective way to win over subordinates, so dazzled are they by your in-depth understanding of their job. Although you are an 'outsider' from above, you are capable of *inside baseball*.

Insider trading

Buying and selling stock on the basis of inside information about a company's performance or intentions. In most countries it is illegal because it distorts the 'fair chance' basis for market speculation, the element that keeps the public capital market going.

In the loop

If you are *in the loop*, you are being informed of a developing situation. Similar to being in the inner circle of the king's court. Conversely, if you are excluded from the loop, you should check for possible career problems, and keep your c.v. up to date.

Intrapreneurship

A spirit of innovation and creativity developed within the walls of an existing company, as distinct from 'entrepreneurship' — the same attitude but practised in new STARTUP COMPANIES.

Intuit

An old verb dating back to the eighteenth century, now resurrected by innovation and creativity consultants to describe a direct, instinctive decision-making process that bypasses normal problem-solving mechanisms. Often used by executives who are too lazy, confused or brilliant to consider the facts. As in 'I couldn't handle the numbers, so I *intuited*'. Considered inelegant, at best.

J

Japan-bashing

Gratuitous abuse hurled at Japan because of trade practices that undercut Western competitors. The truly zealous *Japan-basher* attacks legitimate Japanese success as vigorously as he would attack such questionable methods as buying market share or living off clandestine subsidies.

Japan, Inc.

The full force of Japanese industrial and marketing strength, organized by a combination of government coercion and a Japanese acceptance of the common cause their companies share: the need to grow internationally through competitive advantage.

Jawboning

Talking your way through a problem through negotiation or exploratory meetings with an adversary. The jawbone does the work, and the growing familiarity with the opposition theoretically makes compromise easier.

J-curve

A trend that drops sharply before recovering just as sharply, forming a vague 'j' shape on a graph. The weakening of a currency should produce a *j-curve* effect on a country's trade balance. If the currency weakens in surges over a long period, the trade figures take on the shape of a 'cascading *j-curve*', or a pattern of many consecutive j-shapes. If the currency finally recovers, the *j-curve* may turn into a HOCKEY STICK.

Jidoka

In manufacturing, the instant surfacing of a problem because it stops the carefully calculated flow of an interlocking process. Borrowed from the Japanese who have made a speciality of spotting such problems. Especially acute when JUST-IN-TIME (JIT) inventory control systems are in use.

JIT

A Japanese method of controlling the flow of materials in a manufacturing process so that each bit arrives on the production line *'just-in-time'* (*JIT*) to be used. The cost of carrying out an expensive inventory of outside materials is thus pushed UPSTREAM to the suppliers, giving the illusion of savings. In reality, *JIT* simply spreads the costs on to the balance sheets of the suppliers. Western manufacturers have had problems adjusting to *JIT*, preferring the time-honoured 'just-in-case' inventory stockpiling method instead.

Jumpstart

Similar to KICKSTART, although normally restricted to cash injections. The allusion is to the interconnection of car batteries via jumper cables, drawing current from a strong battery to start the engine of a disabled car.

Just-in-time

See JIT.

K

Kanban

Often wrongly used by the non-Japanese as a synonym for JUST-IN-TIME (JIT) inventory control systems. Actually, *kanban* simply means 'display card'. It was Taiichi Ohno of Toyota who developed the use of display cards to track materials so closely through the manufacturing process that reordering could be done 'just in time' to put the materials to use.

Kickstart

A sudden management initiative (usually cash or a new strategy) designed to produce immediate results. But as in the motorcycle world (whence the term originates), attempting to KICKSTART a machine that is not in working order is a futile pursuit. (See also JUMPSTART.)

Kill

Used as a noun, this is a synonym in some aggressive companies for 'sale' or 'deal'. Such is the pressure in these firms that customers are viewed as targets, the salesmen are cast as hunters, and the sales pitch becomes the ammunition. It is all very macho, even for the women. When a deal is closed, the customer is '*killed*' by the keen aim of the salesman/hunter. From these types, you will hear occasional yelps such as 'I have a *kill*!' Good salespeople have a good success rate, or '*kill* ratio'.

Killer bee

An advisor, usually a lawyer, who helps a company devise a strategy to repel a PREDATOR in a take-over attempt.

Kiting

The practice of writing cheques greater than your bank balance, then depositing funds to cover the cheque before the cheque passes from retailer through the cheque clearing system to the bank.

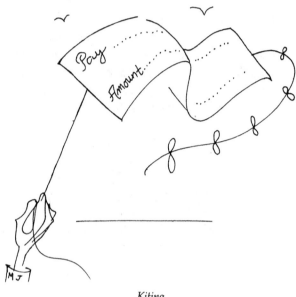

Kiting

Knowledge engineering

The practice of maintaining and improving the skills of your workforce at all levels as your industry's technology develops in new ways. Neglect is as fatal as would be the incompetent engineering of your products.

KITA

A management style that demands action from subordinates, using a figurative 'Kick In the Arse' if necessary.

L

Laundering

Disguising the origin or trail of money by depositing it in foreign banks, then withdrawing it or moving it to other foreign banks until your home-country authorities are unable to trace it.

Layered

What has happened to you when your responsibilities are eroded by a new layer of management created above you. Your title and salary remain the same, but your job is diminished. Usually a good time to update your c.v.

Leadership

A combination of skills and intangible strengths that instills confidence in employees or subordinates. Some elements of *leadership* can be learned, but not by everyone. Studies of *leadership* qualities indicate that some men and women are born with the gift of *leadership*. (See also CHARISMA.)

Leads and lags

In economics, the predictable lapse of time in an interrelated chain of developments. *Leading* indicators such as housing starts may help predict a coming economic expansion. When currency is devalued, a *lag* of 12–18 months may ensue before exports make measurable gains.

Learning curve

The rate of improvement in performing a new job. A key to

industrial costs in companies that require complex work from production-line employees, as in the semiconductor industry. By extension, the pace of assimilation of all aspects of any new position, including executive posts.

Left brain

A person who is strong in organizational skills, proficient in mathematics, and probably obsessed with order and structure. An executive who says 'I hate surprises' is a *left brain* kind of guy. The opposite of RIGHT BRAIN. (See also QUANT.)

Legs

That special endurance of an advertising campaign, movie, book, or other normally short-life product that sells and sells beyond all expectation.

Legwork

The collection of data or information the hard way, by going from source to source. Originally it referred to the newspaperman's job, performed by a legman.

Letter quality

See DAISY WHEEL.

Level playing field

This is what Europeans and Americans often claim they lack when trying to compete with Japanese and other Asian companies. The *'playing field'* is the trading environment, and the rules are said to be artificially tilted in favour of the Asians. For example, Asians can sell in our markets, but we have problems selling in theirs. In truth, the game is made all the more dangerous when the Asians do succeed in producing higher quality at lower prices, winning in any marketplace, whatever the degree or direction of the tilt.

Leveraged buy-in

The purchase of a company by outside managers who put up some of their money but borrow most of it from banks or venture capitalists. The deal is *leveraged* in that the managers' stake can move dramatically upwards or just as dramatically into deficit as they develop or destroy the business. A variation on the more common leveraged buy-out, which is usually engineered from inside.

Levers

Business management lingo for the range of initiatives available at the executive level to influence operations. Managers speak in terms of *levers* of power, as they examine their unseen options for causing quite tangible results. A *lever* for a quick correction of a sudden drop in profit might be a staff cut. Pushing and pulling the right *levers* at the right time is what management is all about.

List rental

The marketing of mailing lists for use by others. The flood of junk mail you throw out every day is generated by the *list-rental* business. Address lists can be purchased for any combination of targeted qualities – wealth, profession, leisure interests, or, as the old joke goes, all left-handed redheads living north of the equator.

Living dead

A STARTUP COMPANY that is about to become profitable, but not very. A favourite concept of the venture capitalists.

Loose-tight

The dual attitude adopted by some innovative companies

seeking a higher level of voluntary commitment from employees. The two elements of the approach are relaxation of control over the individual, but tightness in financial control. Some consultants argue that this *loose-tight* combination is the most effective management style for this era of BOTTOM-LINE pressures and concern for human values.

Loss leader

The underpriced item in your store or in your catalogue that lures buyers in to browse, during which they fall prey to impulse, and end up purchasing several overpriced items as well.

Low-ball pricing

The practice of undercutting your competitors' prices, even if it costs you money temporarily.

Lumpy demand

A market with 'lumps' in its performance curve due to seasonal variables, geographical differences, or the imponderables of changing consumer taste.

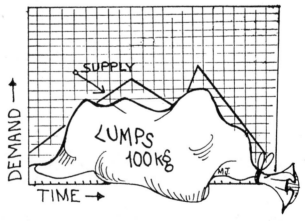

Lumpy demand

M

Mail shot

Direct marketers' terminology for dumping thousands of pieces of junk mail unrequested on people who fit a targeted profile. Returns are sometimes considered 'successful' in response volume as small as a fraction of one per cent, the other 99 per cent having rejected the pitch.

Making your numbers

An absolute requirement in BOTTOM LINE companies, *making your numbers* means meeting or exceeding the numerical targets you agreed to at the beginning of the year. Some executives pride themselves on their record of *making numbers*. Some will put this objective above all others, however, starving research and development, cutting the marketing budget, or taking other shortcuts that undermine the long-term viability of the business. In *making their numbers*, they harm the business.

Management by exception

The art of keeping hands off the business at all times except when data or other circumstances indicate anomalies are developing. Until or unless the anomalies surface, each layer of management is allowed to manage itself.

Management guru

See GURU.

Market-driven

A company that plans its strategy according to information

from the market-place. Great effort goes into studying market trends. See also CUSTOMER-DRIVEN.

Market-hopping

The practice of adjusting your global investment portfolio by selling your stocks in country A in order to buy in country B.

Market meltdown

Armageddon in the stock exchange. *Meltdown* is an evocative, if inappropriate, term from the nuclear power industry designating a chain reaction so far out of control that it melts everything around it. No reactor, not even Chernobyl, has yet melted down. Unchecked, the reactor theoretically would develop a 'China syndrome', meaning the molten metal would sink through the earth and out the other side.

Market meltdown

Marzipan set

A tasty entry from the cookbook, these are the people in an organization who are above the great mass of workers but beneath the top level of management. By extension, now beginning to show up as a sub-speciality of the HEADHUNTING profession — those who recruit middle management, but won't touch secretarial services or the real icing on the corporate cake. If the term ever gets into the French language, it will be *'Les pâtes d'amandes'*. But then things always sound better in French.

Massaging the numbers

'Massage' in the sense of gentle coaxing or reshaping. In business, especially stretching or contracting sums on a balance sheet or business plan to make the mathematics come out right. The term sometimes connotes shady financial practices.

Massaging the numbers

Matrix printer

Computer printer technology consisting of a grid of dots activated to form letters in high-speed printing. (See also DOT MATRIX.)

Mature

A *mature* company is one that has exhausted its capacity to enjoy a free ride on the expansion of its industry. This problem can be caused by saturation of the market by the *mature* company, or a flattening of growth in the industry as a whole. *Mature* companies need new strategies that will take market share from competitors or move the business into diversifications.

Maximax

The GAME THEORY strategy of maximizing the chances of the maximum result.

Maximin

The GAME THEORY strategy for maximizing the chance of minimum loss.

MBWA

A FLAT PYRAMID style of management that calls for executives to get out of their offices and mix with employees. Variously defined as 'Management By Walking Around' and 'Management By Wandering About.' Credited to John Young, chairman of Hewlett-Packard, as its leading practitioner.

Megabid

A large price offered for a company. As a rough measure, the offer should be above $2.5 billion to qualify. The term is part of the cancerous spread of 'mega' as a prefix to describe bigness. Also popular as megabucks, megamerger and, after the celebration, megahangover.

MEGO effect

The impact on an audience made by an inept presenter. When your listeners begin staring vacant-eyed into space, they are under the MEGO spell. Acronym for 'My Eyes Glazed Over'.

Mentoring

The benevolent supervision of a subordinate's career by a senior executive. More formalized in some companies than in others, but generally accepted everywhere as an effective way to give promising young executives a personal touch in their otherwise anxious corporate lives. Taken from Mentor, a character in Homer's *The Odyssey* – a story that is a fitting metaphor for many corporate careers.

Metaphor

A qualitative research technique for exploring consumers' feelings about a product or service. The consumer might be asked to think of an animal as a *metaphor* for the product – a vacuum cleaner as a goat, for example – and to describe it in detail.

Me-too product

An imitation, sometimes with minor refinements, of a product already in the market-place. Each new imitator, when told that a competitor has such a product, can thus retort, '*Me too.*'

Milken

A unit of financial measure equal to $500 million. The term can be heard occasionally in high-flying money circles on Wall Street. Thus a takeover bid in the billion-dollar range is worth 2 *Milkens*. The $500 million basic figure is said to have been the annual compensation of former Drexel Burnham 'junk bond' impresario Michael Milken. The *Milken* is a contemporary version of the old Texas oilmen's 'Unit', which is $100 million. On a more modest scale, the London advertising fraternity has its 'Seymour', only £100,000, referring to the salary offered Geoffrey Seymour of Saatchi and Saatchi in the early 1980s. Since then, numerous admen have moved into the 2-Seymour category and beyond.

Mindset

A person's attitude or way of looking at the world – assumptions and preconceptions usually different from your own. 'He's an engineer. You have to understand his *mindset.*' The term sprang up from nowhere in the 1980s and spread like a 'flu virus.

Minimax

In GAME THEORY, a strategy minimizing the risk of suffering maximum loss.

Misery index

In times of high inflation and unemployment, a chart that tracks those two trends.

More bang for the buck

An objective of companies that want to obtain better return (*bang*) on their investment (*buck*). Originally computer jargon to indicate more power per dollar. Slang at its worst, and not recommended in situations where English is not everyone's mother tongue.

Movers and shakers

The important people; the men and women who make things happen.

Mr Inside

In entrepreneurial companies, the partner with the most expertise, often technical know-how, in developing the products and the business. His main partner, also necessary to the firm's survival, is MR OUTSIDE.

Mr Outside

The partner in a new venture who is most effective with bankers and venture capitalists. (See also the other required half of the management team, MR INSIDE.)

MRP

A computerized approach to keeping track of raw materials, components and sub-assemblies in a manufacturing process. *MRP* (for Materials Requirement Planning) was considered the panacea of the 1970s but failed to live up to its promise. In recent years, successor systems have competed for the attention and investment of companies striving for that elusive ideal of perfect efficiency in manufacturing.

Multi-dimensional decision-making

The practice of analysing a situation in all its aspects before taking a decision. Recent research shows that the more levels of analysis, the better the decision. The catch is that executives who manage this way are more prone to heart attacks. In other words, the better you manage, the sooner you are going to die.

Murphia

The Irish expatriates' self-help system – a sort of benign version of the Sicilian Mafia. Few expatriate groups look out for each other's interests as effectively as the Irish: networking for jobs, sharing in sales opportunities, moral support, is all part of the Irish scene abroad. Inevitably, the common Irish surname 'Murphy' became merged with the Sicilian 'Mafia'. The Welsh (known as 'Taffies') have a similar network abroad, the Taffia.

Mushroom management

A management technique that consists of keeping employees in the dark and feeding them liberal doses of organic fertilizer. Not a good idea.

Mushroom management

Mystery shopping

Study of retail conditions by professionals posing as ordinary consumers. After a *mystery shopping* expedition, reports are produced on how a designated product is being presented by sales clerks, retail managers and other sales personnel.

N

Name of the game

An expression from the 1960s that means 'the heart of the matter'. In business, the *name of the game* varies from company to company. Some firms would say employee fulfilment, satisfaction and security are the *name of the game*. But the honest ones would acknowledge that it is profit. In publicly traded companies, it is fashionable and safer to say 'maximizing shareholder wealth' is the *name of the game*.

Narrowcasting

Paid commercials on radio or television aimed at a small segment of the broad audience actually being reached. Thus a commercial message aimed at doctors might be carried on a popular radio station at a time of day that doctors are presumed to be listening. More or less the opposite of 'broadcasting'.

National champion

The country's primary supplier of a technology or product; often the beneficiary of indirect government subsidies such as lucrative research contracts or guaranteed orders through the public procurement system. A corporate form threatened with extinction in Europe as protectionism among the European Community members declines and Europe-wide partnerships develop.

Negative cashflow

A euphemism for the financial condition of a loss-making company. Tolerable to a business if temporary, as in the case of a start-up phase or CYCLICALITY, but fatal if allowed to persist. In terminal cases, the technical ring of the phrase makes it easier to live with than the more straightforward, 'I'm heading for bankruptcy.'

Negative corporate worth

The sad state of affairs when the divisions or subsidiaries of a large company actually suffer, rather than benefit, from being part of the group. When unsure, try the formula used by take-over artists and ASSET-STRIPPERS: evaluate the parts of a corporation, and if the sum of the parts is greater than the worth of the whole company, you have *negative corporate worth*. Obviously a danger sign for top management.

Negative raider

Financial manipulator so feared and so powerful that he causes as much disruption when he withdraws his holdings as when he places them. Sir James Goldsmith recently earned this nickname when he dramatically reduced his investments in companies in the United States and France.

Nemawashi

The process of consensus-building in Japanese companies. By extension, laying the groundwork for any initiative. This term is borrowed from bonsai tree cultivation, where it means the art of binding roots together. Curiously, in horticulture it is designed to stunt growth, but in business it is intended to *ensure* growth through harmony.

Nerd

A person with limited perspective and a minimum of charm

Nemawashi

(except among other *nerds*). Especially prevalent among computer enthusiasts. (See also COMPUTER NERD, NERDPACK.)

Nerdpack

A pocketful of coloured pens neatly held in a plastic sheath and worn – like a badge – in the shirt pocket. NERDPACKS are for engineers and computer programmers who have earned their status as NERDS, or compulsive-obsessive gadget freaks.

Nester

An old-fashioned consumer who is unmoved by advertising hype, preferring instead traditional family values and products that deliver value for money.

Networking

Staying in touch with people likely to be useful in your career development. Business schools, religious groups, ex-employees of certain large corporations, all maintain 'alumni clubs'. Members favour each other in all manner of business situations. If you are not part of a *network*, you are probably at a career disadvantage.

Niche

A small, cosy place in the market where a relatively small business can be built without much danger of being disturbed. *Niche player* is the common term for the company in such a business. Usually pronounced the French way, *neesh*, which happens to mean doghouse.

Nickel-and-diming

American slang for harassment by accountants over small sums. Nickels and dimes are small-denomination US coins. Typical moaning by victims of such harassment would be: 'I'm being *nickel-and-dimed* to death.' A painful way to go.

Nifty fifty

Wall Street slang for the hottest 50 stocks among the big institutional investors.

NIH syndrome

The rejection of an idea on the grounds that it cannot possibly be of value if it comes from outside. This is one of the fundamental blockages to innovation in large, complacent companies. *NIH* stands for 'Not Invented Here'. In such companies, very little is.

NLQ

Computer printer typeface based on MATRIX technology

which types over each letter twice, improving the result to *Near Letter Quality* (*NLQ*). (See also DAISY WHEEL.)

No-brainer

Derogatory language for another person's idea or proposal – one that you think so worthless or silly as to be brainless.

NOLAD

Marketing acronym for Non-Listening Attention Demand, the pull of distractions in radio listening habits. A housewife washing dishes has a low *NOLAD* rating, but a driver with a load of noisy passengers has a high rating. Radio advertisers know that listeners' *NOLAD* ratings swing wildly throughout the day, and they hate it.

Non-starter

A proposal without a future, an idea with no audience, a concept that won't work. Try something else.

Number-crunching

The process of analysing numerical data, usually by computer.

O

Obituary technique

When market researchers seek consumers' deepest feelings about a product by asking them to write obituaries of the item, describing its 'life' and its cause of 'death'. Morbid, perhaps, but effective.

Obscuranto

Foggy bureaucratic jargon in international organizations. The language of such organizations goes limp from too many committee members putting their stamp on each pronouncement. This term is most commonly used in Brussels to refer to documents originating at the European Commission. It is a facetious combination of 'obscure' and 'Esperanto'.

Office bicycle

The girl in the office who is most popular with the men.

OINK

One of the increasingly common acronyms floating around these days to designate one's professional and/or marital status. This one means 'One income, No Kids.' From the same linguistic orphanage as DINKY (Double Income, No Kids Yet), and SWELL (Single Woman Earning Lots in London).

Old old

The most advanced age group that marketing experts attempt to target: the over 75s. (See also YOUNG OLD.)

Oink

On a roll

The condition of a company that is hurtling forward with the speed of a loose wheel bouncing downhill. It is exhilarating if you can avoid the trees.

On a roll

On line

A computer is *on line* when connected to a mainframe or to another PC. Not quite the same as UP AND RUNNING. In manufacturing, a synonym for ON STREAM.

On stream

A plant that is operational is said to be on stream. The stream it is on is the flow of materials in one end and products out the other. (See also ON LINE.)

Open outcry

A method of trading in many of the world's commodity or options markets. This is what dealers are doing when they shout, jostle and gesture from the trading floor. The practice is much less violent than it appears on television.

Open probe

In market research, a question that invites an expansive reply. 'Why?' is an *open probe*. The opposite of CLOSED PROBE.

Organic growth

The expansion of business through internal development, rather than through acquisition. Japanese companies have shown special strengths in *organic growth* as they find new ways to put excess manpower to work, sometimes by launching entirely unrelated businesses.

Organogram

A chart showing the lines of reporting among managers, divisions or departments in a company. Charts that tend towards the horizontal usually indicate a democratic management style. Vertical shapes indicate TOP-DOWN management.

Outplacement

Consultants specializing in finding jobs for recently sacked professionals. *Outplacement* fees are normally paid by the sackee's ex-company. *Outplacement* counsellors are often trained psychologists whose first objective is to restore the victim's self-esteem.

Outsourcing

The purchase of components outside your company rather than making them yourself. The advantage is freeing your own company to concentrate on the fabrication of the final product, while allowing others to solve the UPSTREAM problems.

OVA

Nothing to do with eggs. It stands for 'Overhead Value Analysis', the latest method for analysing the cost of overheads, mainly people costs, and deciding where to cut. Another euphemism for axe-wielding.

Overclaim

In market research, the temptation of consumers to please the interviewer by claiming to have used a product or spent more on a product than is actually the case. (See also PRESTIGE EFFECT.)

Overstored

Retail chains find themselves in this predicament when they have expanded too wildly, or are trapped in a sudden downturn, burdened with too many unprofitable outlets. This is much worse than being understored, which at least does not drain resources.

Ozone friendly

To tap into environment-sensitive customers' pocketbooks, clever marketing minds have come up with this term to designate any product that once used chlorofluorocarbons (as in the propellant for aerosols) but no longer does. *Ozone friendly* products do not damage the ozone layer of the earth's atmosphere.

P

Paperless society

One of those futures that never happened. Computer-makers in the 1970s predicted that the spread of their word-processing technology would eliminate the need for paper. After an initial fright, paper manufacturers discovered that demand for paper became even greater as users spewed out more words, printing most of them out on continuous-feed paper with perforated margins. The paper companies quickly shifted from typewriter paper to computer paper, curiously called 'listing paper'.

Paradigm

Once a perfectly good, if pretentious, word meaning 'pattern' or 'role model', from the Greek *paradeigma*. It caused no one harm as long as it was confined to the writings of college professors. But now it has become standard in business school, and graduates are carrying it into the boardroom.

Parallel labour

The untaxed, unrecorded work performed in the parallel economy, or BLACK ECONOMY. *Parallel labour* is the result of a conspiracy between employers and employees against the government. It circumvents taxation, safety and environmental standards and other regulations that may be considered inconvenient.

Pareto Principle

Named for the Italian economist Vilfredo Pareto (1848–1923), the *Pareto Principle* holds that the people who make a difference in a company account for a small percentage of the total. Thus 10 per cent of the employees may account for 90 per cent of the new ideas generated. Determining these proportions can be a key control mechanism for top management. Also known as Pareto's Law and the Pareto Curve.

Parking

The sometimes illegal practice of concealing ownership of equities by temporarily depositing them in the accounts of friends or conspirators. Stock market regulators in some countries take this practice as clear evidence of wrongdoing.

Passalong rate

In newspaper and magazine publishing, the number of people who read each issue. A *passalong rate* of five is good; 10 is outstanding. Advertisers value this figure highly, as it gives them a clearer picture of total readership.

PCNs

In multinational companies, all those employees wordwide who enjoy an unspoken advantage because they are parent-company nationals (*PCNs*). They are favoured over 'foreigners' because of cultural and linguistic affinities. One must, in a British company, appreciate the ins and outs of cricket, for example.

Peak shaving

In any business with inconvenient peaks and valleys to deal with, life can be made more orderly if the peaks are shaved and the valleys filled in. *Peak shaving* is the art of levelling supply and demand.

People meters

The STATE OF THE ART in television audience measurement systems, *people meters* do better than the old Nielsen black box that simply recorded how long a television set was on, and to which channel it was tuned. *People meters*, pioneered by AGB Research in Britain, attempt to determine whether anyone is actually watching the programmes. Each family member has a button to press while watching. Properly used, the system provides far more accurate and detailed data on viewer habits and choices.

Peter Principle

The inevitable arrival of an employee at a career level too demanding for his or her talents. Career momentum often propels the strong performers into more responsible jobs beyond their abilities. Result: disaster for the executive, a HICCUP for the company. Coined by the late Prof. Laurence Peter, a Canadian-born US academic.

Pick and shovel work

In the language of lawyers and accountants, the line-by-line examination of documents to ensure their perfection. Dull and boring to normal people, but a real treat for a true numbers person or the dedicated legal mind.

Pie chart

An American and British term for graphic representation of percentages as 'slices' of a circle. To a Frenchman, cultural conditioning gives the same chart the name CAMEMBERT.

Pig in a python

Graphic metaphor common among marketing theorists and

demographers to describe the bulge in the birthrate between 1946 and 1964, the so-called baby boom years. Product developers follow the *'pig'* as it moves along the *'python'* of steady population growth, creating and easing demand as age groups expand and contract.

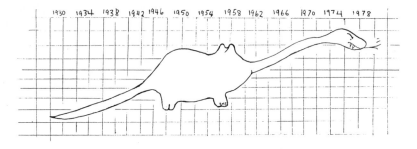

Pig in a python

Pink slip

The cowardly way some companies have of informing employees they are being dismissed. Like 'green cards', which are no longer green, *pink slips* now come in all colours. (See also PINK SLIPPERS.)

Pink slippers

Those who have received PINK SLIPS, or termination notices. The term dates back to America of the 1930s, when company practice was to sack employees in a terse memo on rose-coloured paper.

Placement company

Firms in television and film-producing capitals that specialize in inserting mention of their clients' products into the scripts of movies and television productions. A highly effective form of hidden advertising, and legal if done openly. French television was shaken by a scandal in the 1970s, however, for *publicité clandestine*, in which the proceeds went to individuals, not to the production company.

Plastic

Slang for credit card or charge card. A card holder might ask a restaurant waiter: 'Do you take *plastic*?'

Player

A term from the sporting world now used in business to designate companies worth taking into account in a competitive situation.

PLC

A controversial use of television time, especially on the under-utilized cable and satellite channels, in which sales messages are disguised as legitimate programming. The material is broadcast as 'Programme Length Commercials'. Thirty minutes on home security, for example, might appear to be a documentary on burglary trends but actually is a soft sell for the paying client's alarm systems. Also in Britain, abbreviation for 'Public Limited Company'.

Plug-compatible

Modules of computer systems that can literally be plugged into modules of certain other manufacturers with whom they are designed to interact. CLONES are *plug-compatible* with the equipment of the model they imitate.

Poaching

Originally the crime of hunting game on someone else's

property, now a slightly different, but more common, practice in companies that need specific skills – raiding the competitor's staff. Being *poached* is flattering except when the *poacher's* aim is as much to harm the competition as to acquire your skills.

Point man

The person designated to manage a strategy or defend a point of view. The *point man* acts as the shock absorber for the company. Often an opportunity for high visibility but a dangerous role. If ineffective, he may be sacrificed.

Poison pill

Debt and other liabilities taken on by companies to corrupt the balance sheet and make the company a less inviting target to RAIDERS. Marginally preferable to disappearing into a hostile suitor's corporation, but beneficial only to the lawyers and financial advisers who arrange for you to swallow it.

Poison pill

Poka-yoke

A feature of a Japanese-made machine designed so that operators cannot possibly utilize it incorrectly. Built-in safeguards make operator errors physically impossible. IDIOT-PROOF, but on a more sophisticated level.

Ponzi Scheme

An investment fraud in which investors in phase one are paid by the funds from a larger phase-two base, who in turn are paid by an even larger phase-three group. Eventually, the chain is exhausted, the scheme has no productive assets, and the last phase of investors remains unpaid. Named for Charles Ponzi, an Italian immigrant to the United States who swindled thousands of Americans in 1919–20 with the classic PYRAMID fraud. His 'business' was trading in International Postal Reply coupons, but in fact he and his early investors pocketed all funds that poured in. His slogan '40 per cent in 90 days' proved irresistible. Ponzi ended up in jail.

Poor excellence

An informal rating created by some executives at IBM Europe in Paris to characterize performance in which effort was commendable but the result left something to be desired.

Popular capitalism

The personal investment phenomenon that Europe finally imported from the United States in the late 1980s, only to discover that a broader base of shareholdings is a mixed blessing. It may help give the population-at-large a sense of ownership in big companies, but it rarely means shelter for hard-won savings. The crash of 1987 was a rude awakening. It resulted in pleas in France for downside protection for the country's new stock market players. Experienced gamblers in the United States and Britain greeted the French fears with hoots of derision.

Powder-room

New meaning for a charming old expression for toilet. Women used to powder their noses there. Today's YUPPIES use the same location to snort cocaine, a very different kind of powder.

Power breakfast

Doing business at sunrise in hotel restaurants, in the same location as other MOVERS AND SHAKERS. The Hotel Pierre in New York now offers 'power tea' in late afternoon.

Predator

A term from the animal kingdom, this is the person or company who pounces on innocent victims and eats them alive. Or are they innocent? Often *predators* have broken up ossified corporate groups and structures that needed a fresh, outside force to breathe life back into them. In such cases, the *predator* becomes the saviour.

Press kit

A 'friendly' name for a folder containing several dozen pages of soft-sell documentation backing up an oral presentation at a press conference. Journalists who fail to show up at press conferences are punished in the next morning's post by the arrival on their desks of these voluminous and largely useless *press kits*.

Prestige effect

Distortions in market research by respondents who wish,

perhaps without acknowledging it to themselves, to supply answers that they believe enhance their own prestige.

Prioritize

One of the most barbarous examples of the American habit of turning nouns into verbs. 'Priority' is a worthy noun: companies and individuals rise and fall on the strength of their ability to set priorities. To *prioritize* is merely a BUZZWORD, and should not be treated as good English. As the Oxford English Dictionary supplement diplomatically puts it: 'A word that at present sits uneasily in the language.'

Privatization

A particularly infelicitous British word invented in the early 1980s to replace 'denationalization', apparently in the belief that *'privatize'* sounds more positive. Confusing in the concept of private vs. public companies, however, as a *privatized* company usually becomes publicly held. To make matters worse, now the French have borrowed it as *privatisation*, although they also had the perfectly good alternative, *dénationalisation*, in their vocabulary.

Product mix

In cyclical industries, the *product mix* is the secret of success: the proper balance of products that might ensure against collapse in one sector's downturn. NICHE players are at a disadvantage in such circumstances because they have no ingredients to mix.

Projective techniques

Research methods for overcoming natural distortions in respondents' answers by going beyond standard question-and-answer techniques. The methods can sometimes reveal hidden feelings about a product or a service. In the United States recently, women who participated in research for an insecticide were asked to draw pictures of cockroaches and discuss the client's product in relation to them. Analysis revealed that the women preferred spray insecticide to other poisons because it enabled them to observe the cockroaches (which represented selfish men) writhing in pain and finally dying. (See also METAPHOR, OBITUARY TECHNIQUES, PSYCHO-DRAMA.)

Psychic income

The satisfaction derived from your job; sometimes almost a substitute for money. Current theories hold that most people are motivated by such factors as the need to make a contribution, the urge to achieve self-esteem, not by money alone. Japanese management concepts, including QUALITY CIRCLES, are typical of *psychic income* schemes. While seemingly less costly than higher wages, they are actually far more difficult to install and manage.

Psychodrama

PROJECTIVE TECHNIQUE for discovering consumers' true attitudes. A *psychodrama* might be a 'conversation' between two products, or a theatrical play enacting a shopping excursion.

Psychographics

The classification of consumers according to attitudes or other psychological attributes. Prevalent in market research. Also known as psychometrics.

Pump Priming

The injection of financial resources to help the business or the economy back on its feet. In a company, *pump priming* might be investment in research or product development. In the economy, it might be expansion of certain kinds of credit.

Puppie

A YUPPIE after he or she has failed. In full, a Previously Young Urban Professional.

Pure play

An investment strategy that concentrates on one product or one industry that the investor feels will carry him forward. A believer in ARTIFICIAL INTELLIGENCE (AI), for example, would make a *pure play* for AI stocks, and wait patiently for the payoff to come.

Pure vanilla

A range of products with nothing but basic characteristics, no frills. Like the simplest flavour of ice cream, it has no excitement.

Pushing the envelope

A term from the aircraft industry, *envelope pushers* are the pilots (now including pilots of companies) who like to test their endurance or breaking point by trying things that would ordinarily be considered beyond the capability of the machine or organization. If the envelope expands, fine; if it rips open, you have overreached.

Pyramid

See PONZI SCHEME.

Q

Quality circles

Japanese-inspired management technique for improving work practices, and therefore productivity and quality, by formalized discussion in small groups. In some companies, practised at all levels. Among Europeans, most widely used in France.

Quant

A numbers man (or woman), a person adept at quantifying all things under the sun. *Quants* usually are trained in mathematics or computer science, and apply their uncompromising skills in the securities industry.

Quick fix

A repair job, usually on a balance sheet, that temporarily solves a problem. Too many *quick fixes* can result in a quick funeral.

Qwerty keyboard

In the computer business, the qwerty keyboard is the model configured for English-language users. The first five letters on the keyboard are Q, W, E, R, T, Y. In French keyboards, the same keys spell AZERTY. In German, QWERTZ.

QWL

Quality of Work Life, a BUZZWORD of the 1980s: the attempt to view work in humane, HOLISTIC terms, taking into account tasks performed, work environment, career development as well as payment for services.

R

Raider

The person who takes the initiative in accumulating stock in a company, with the apparent intention of buying control. Often the *raider* pulls out before consummation is reached, and cashes in his gains from the rise in stock prices he caused.

Rainmaker

A colourful figure of speech to describe the ultimate in management talent, the man (occasionally, the woman) who can make the impossible happen in your company, even make the clouds open up. Executive search firms use it as part of their normal vocabulary.

Ratchet

A verb describing the step-by-step movement of numbers, usually higher. Most commonly used in the sense of salaries, prices or inflation rates *ratcheting* upwards.

Razor and blade

A pricing strategy for products that require a replacement element. The model is the cheap razor and the expensive blade. Westinghouse tried it on the grandest scale ever, in the nuclear power industry, building reactors on a low profit margin, intending to make a killing on uranium sales. Both ends of the business collapsed in the 1970s, well before the payback started.

Reading the desk

Salesmen do this while they're still shaking hands in a prospect's office. *Reading the desk* entails a quick survey of personal mementoes and other items that might open a friendly, non-threatening kind of chitchat before the sales pitch begins. Then recalling such details for future contact is a standard salesman's trick for ingratiating himself with the would-be client.

Read my lips

American slang that roughly means 'If you cannot grasp the message I am giving you, listen harder.' George Bush gave the term currency when voters doubted his pledge that he would not raise US taxes. In effect, he was saying he really meant it. People still didn't believe him.

Real-world anthropology

A new science from the United States focusing on corporate culture but using the techniques of anthropology to study it. The object is to distinguish the company's view of what it is doing from what it is actually doing. The gulf is sometimes formidable.

Receivables

Money owed to a company, and carried on the books as such. Collecting the *receivables* is another matter.

Received wisdom

See CONVENTIONAL WISDOM.

Recency bias

A tendency of respondents in market studies to show more enthusiasm or knowledge of a product recently used. A good questionnaire will identify *recency bias* by asking timeframe questions such as 'When did you last sample the product?'

Red bits

International marketspeak in Britain that designates the former British colonies around the globe. Thus a new product might be destined for 'the home market and the *red bits*'. The term comes from British school maps in which the once-great Empire was always coloured in red.

Red flag

A danger sign. A high defect rate is a *red flag* for a manufacturing company.

Refolution

New trends sometimes require new words. Refolution is a hybrid of 'reform' and 'revolution'. A *refolution* that almost happened was the China experiment with free speech. Others that are still trying to happen are the *glasnost-perestroika* movements in the Soviet Union.

Reinventing the wheel

Developing products or conducting studies that duplicate work already done by others. A MINDSET of the arrogant or ignorant.

Repositioning

Moving a product about in the competitive spectrum to attain a more advantageous position. If competition is too vicious at the TOP OF THE LINE, a manufacturer might remove his product's frills and relaunch at a cheaper price. The marketing, distribution and customers all become different and, the manufacturer hopes, more responsive.

Resonance

The impact of an idea as it races through your company, triggering sympathetic reactions. This is a trendy coinage now cropping up in management writings and in conversation among the *cognoscenti*. Only the good ideas achieve *resonance*. The rest die in the mental soundproofing of the executive suite.

Revenue stream

A vivid metaphor for visualizing another abstraction of business — the flow of cash from specific products or profit centres. To help equalize the cycles that plague some businesses, new *revenue streams* attuned to opposite cycles are constantly being sought.

Reverse engineering

Analysis of a competitor's product by dismantling it and studying the design and components. A top-priority activity in the computer industry each time a rival unveils a product with a new array of capabilities. If nothing else, this process guarantees each new product a few dozen quick orders.

RIF

Reduction In Force; payroll cutback.

Right brain

An individual whose strengths are on the creative side.

Reverse engineering

Recent brain research indicates the creative, emotional sides of the personality are concentrated in the right side of the brain. (See also LEFT BRAIN.)

Rip off

To steal in a public, shameless fashion. In business, *ripping off* of ideas is a daily occurrence. When a noun, written as one word: 'That campaign is a *ripoff* of ours from last year.' (See also RIPOFF ARTIST.)

Ripoff artist

A strategist, product designer, consultant, or any individual adept at stealing, usually ideas.

Robinson Crusoe Week

One of those weeks in the year that includes a major market-moving announcement scheduled for Friday. Investors hold back decisions 'waiting for Friday'.

Rocket scientist

The brainiest of the management team – the person who is clever enough to build a rocket to the moon, but in fact is called upon only to produce black ink on the balance sheet.

Rollout

The launch or first presentation of a product, even if it has no wheels. Originally an aerospace term for presenting aircraft to the public. Now, by extension, any product introduction.

Roundtable

An open discussion of problems or opportunities, usually by representatives from different companies. The actual table may not be round, but the idea of roundness means that everyone speaks as an equal.

Rubber rate cards

In advertising sales, overcoming rigidity; the practice of discounting as often as necessary in order to sell pages.

Rust belt

The US phenomenon of decline in heavy industry, most of which was concentrated in the Midwest. Rust belt problems sparked a move to the South, which became the Sunbelt. Both phenomena are coming to Europe as the industrial powerhouses of Northern Europe, especially in the German Ruhr Valley, Scotland and the north of England, suffer decline as the economic growth rates of sunnier climates such as Spain and Portugal rise sharply.

S

Sackable offence

In the language of personnel professionals, the mishaps that company policy would automatically consider serious enough for termination.

Scam

An American expression of uncertain origin meaning a dishonest scheme.

Scapegoating

In a quick reshuffle of people or policy, it is always handy to have a *scapegoat* to help explain why the previous set-up wasn't working. The original scapegoat came from Mosaic law in which the Hebrews sent a goat into the wilderness symbolically carrying away the burden of a tribe's sins. Today the word is increasingly used as a verb in the language of corporate change.

Scenario

A technique of business forecasting developed into a fine art by Royal Dutch/Shell. A team of specialists from several disciplines examines known data and hypotheses for the future, and produces *scenarios* of different possible outcomes.

Schadenfreude

A German term, with no equivalent in English, for taking pleasure in another's misfortune. In business, a common character flaw among the fiercely competitive.

Scope out

An engineering term, derived from 'oscilloscope' and changed into a verb, that means to analyse or to find a solution. To *scope out* implies a major feat of logical deduction.

Scratch and sniff

A printing technique that bonds and seals a scent onto paper. The consumer is then invited to *scratch and sniff*. Another idea from America.

Screwdriver operations

Manufacturing facilities that perform only simple assembly work 'with a screwdriver'. Usually a pejorative that designates US or Japanese plants in Europe where no technology transfer is included, requiring only the lowest form of unskilled labour.

Secular trends

In economics, the record of a national economy over a long period.

Seed corn

A synonym for SEED MONEY.

Seed money

In venture capital, the investment in a STARTUP COMPANY before there is any prospect of profit. The venture capitalist thinks of his *seed money* like a farmer thinks of his spring planting. With the right conditions, it will grow to maturity and be harvested. Sometimes in venture capital the conditions can change as quickly and erratically as the weather.

SEL

Acronym for secured employment level, a new bargaining objective of US trade unions working to stop the reduction of payroll during a sales downturn or a productivity increase. With no *SELs*, the trade union is doomed to shrink.

Serious money

Quantities of money sufficient to make a difference after tax. A favourite term in financial institutions, where salaries tend to reach *'serious'* proportions very quickly. So widely used that a London play dramatizing the fast life of the financial whiz borrowed the term as its title.

Seven sisters

The oil majors: Exxon, Royal Dutch/Shell, Mobil, Socal, Texaco, British Petroleum and Gulf (now absorbed in Socal).

Sexy

One of the most curious of all business BUZZWORDS, this is a rare example of a term that has been desexed by usage. *Sexy* products, *sexy* strategies or *sexy* stories are simply thought to be more interesting and more original than unsexy ones. Perhaps at one time the implication was that the product, strategy or story was as intriguing as the difference between the sexes.

Share of mind

A key factor in achieving success in brand recognition. Market share is important to have, but the more elusive *share of mind* tells you how deep the consumer's commitment is. Once *share of mind* is achieved, share of market will follow. The problem is measuring it.

Shark repellent

Anti-*predator* strategies in a hostile take-over bid. (See also KILLER BEE, POISON PILL.)

Shop floor

In manufacturing, the part of the company where the dirty work is done. Only eccentric white-collar managers used to be seen there. Nowadays in the age of FLATTER PYRAMIDS, the *shop floor* is crawling with white shirts.

Shop talk

The discussion of the day's business after working hours. WORKAHOLICS are inveterate shop-talkers. Too much *shop talk* probably indicates an individual's limitations. It is a curse of the YUPPIE generation, although not exclusive to them. A professional wrestler might tell his wife: 'I throwed a big bruiser today,' while the chairman of a consumer goods group is telling his wife: 'I finally sacked Reggie today.' In both cases, the wife dutifully feigns interest.

Short-termism

The attitude that is probably ruining the US economy, to wit, using company assets to generate short-term profit while sacrificing long-term investment. Carried to an extreme, obviously a recipe for starving a company to death. Capital markets demand short-term return, however, so many managers are caught between that need and the ultimate survival of the company. Wise executives learn how to persuade investors that survival is at least as important as next quarter's results.

Shotgun

A style of marketing effort without demographic focus. A *shotgun* campaign aims wide and hopes for the best.

Shrinkage

The loss of inventory in the retail business through shoplifting and staff pilferage. *EPOS* systems have helped large retail groups measure the extent of their shrinkage problem for the first time, with results that were much to their horror.

SIB

The new Securities and Investment Board, which has overall responsibility for regulating the investment industry. Part of Britain's Financial Services Act.

Silent partner

A partner in a company who takes no active part in the management and may not be publicly associated with the enterprise. Also known as a SLEEPING PARTNER.

Sinatra Doctrine

When the Soviet Union abandoned the Brezhnev Doctrine guaranteeing hard-line East European regimes Soviet protection, the *Sinatra Doctrine* emerged in its place. Suddenly every East European is free to evolve 'my way', as in the popular song of the same name performed by crooner Frank Sinatra.

Sizzle

An American expression for the hyped-up image created around a product to make it enticing. The style, as distinct from the substance. (See also STEAK.)

Skunkworks

A flexible work arrangement under which teams of creative

workers are allowed to come and go as they please, with access to laboratories and offices round the clock. The theory is that creative juices flow at unpredictable times. Regimenting your creative people with rigid working hours restricts the 'space' they require. The *skunk* element comes from the fact that the creative staff tend to be nocturnal animals, like skunks. The term was brought to public attention by Thomas Peters and Robert Waterman in their book *In Search of Excellence*.

Slave

A computer terminal or other part of the electronic data processing system that is capable only of obeying commands from an 'intelligent' part of the system.

Sleeper

A product — a book, a movie, any consumer item — that has little initial impact but 'wakes up' later in its life cycle and becomes a success.

Sleeper question

In a research questionnaire, an apparently innocent question that actually reveals whether the respondent is being candid or honest.

Sleeping partner

See SILENT PARTNER.

Smart

Machines that can be programmed to perform complex tasks, as in robotics. *Smart* is an American word for 'intelligent'.

This meaning was accepted with difficulty in Britain, where *smart* means well-groomed, well-dressed or aesthetically well-designed.

Smart card

Wallet-sized cards with embedded integrated circuitry capable of holding data in memory. *Smart cards* are widely used in France as part of a system that debits consumers' bank accounts directly at the retail level, and updates the card to reflect the balance remaining. They are being used experimentally elsewhere in the world by major credit card companies.

Snakecheck

A military practice consisting of a thorough shakeout of backpack and bedding after a night in the field to rid equipment of snakes that might have moved in. US General Alexander Haig popularized the term in politics and business, applying the same thorough attitudes in checking such things as press releases and memos.

Soft option

The path of least resistance, and sometimes the solution of least effect. Managers are often faced with a variety of ways of dealing with a problem. The hard option is the one that involves hurting people. The *soft option* probably only postpones the pain.

Sonking

Derived from the Scientification of Knowledge, a ploy of unethical researchers who clothe their theories or numbers in pseudo-scientific language and theory to give them an air of legitimacy.

Sound bites

Those well-formed sentences on TV news interviews that say so much in so few words, or seem to. Executives who deal with TV reporters must learn to speak in this strange, clipped manner.

Spear carrier

Second-tier representatives of top management; glorified errand boys. In all kinds of business deals, it can be good psychology for the chieftain to stay at home most of the time, allowing the *spear carriers* to conduct limited business – negotiations, stonewalling or anything likely to be unpopular. The chieftain emerges theatrically for the climactic phase.

Spear carrier

Spider organization

Typical of family companies, this is the organization chart in which the founder or owner sits in the middle and extends his or her many tentacles to each manager in the company. The owner thus is the centre of the universe, encircled by subordinates and utterly incapable of managing effectively.

Spin control

The fine art of managing the effects of a major policy change or other pronouncement as it takes on a life of its own. A chairman might declare that his company has reached maturity and as from tomorrow will become decentralized and entrepreneurial. As the employees whirl about, distraught over their future, good *spin control* can help keep the anxiety level down.

Spin-in

An impractical result from the research and development laboratory; the opposite of SPIN-OFF. Many R&D labs are burdened with *spin-in* projects waiting for a market to materialize. But the best R&D teams can sense the moment a *spin-in* is taking shape, and they know how to abort.

Spin-off

A business or part of a business that has grown strong enough to become a STAND-ALONE unit. When it reaches the point of achieving independence, the centrifugal force of its energy *'spins it off'* into its own orbit.

Splurge generation

A new phenomenon in the spending patterns in the over-50s generation, recently spotted by market researchers.

Formerly, this age group was slowing down in spending terms, entering a state of 'junk population' as viewed by marketeers. Today, the over-50s are bent on enjoying their money regardless of tomorrow's problems or their children's financial needs. Marketing types are sitting up and taking notice.

Square one

The beginning, back where you started, the place you landed after your last major disaster. The phrase comes from board games in which players hop from square to square, sometimes forward, sometimes all the way back to *square one*.

SRO

If you are doing business in Britain, this is more than 'Standing Room Only' conditions at West End theatres. *SRO*s are 'Self Regulatory Organizations' in financial services. The five *SRO*s are the Securities Association, the Investment Management Regulatory Organization, the Association of Futures Brokers Dealers, the Financial Intermediaries, the Managers and Brokers Regulatory Organization. They are midway between voluntary associations and statutory bodies.

Stabbing in the front

What happens in companies when the going gets really tough. The ultimate extension of unscrupulous political infighting, or stabbing in the back.

Stalking horse

In the take-over game, the company that starts the bidding for a prey. When the time is right, a stronger PREDATOR may emerge and snatch the prey. The stronger PREDATOR has used the first bidder as a *stalking horse*.

Stabbing in the front

Stand-alone

A business or a system that can function independently of a master.

Startup company

A recently formed business undergoing rapid cycles of panic and euphoria as it seeks new markets, tries to hold finance together and works the BUGS out of its products. *Startups* have their own special feel. Typically they are small, entrepreneurial, optimistic, often boastful, frequently short-lived.

State of the art

The '*art*' is the technology, and the technology is in constant change. Products that are up to date represent the present state of the technology, thus the *state of the art*. This expression is a way of adding a dimension of beauty to what is actually an engineering discipline.

Steak

The true substance of a product or service, as distinct from the style, or SIZZLE. The *steak* and SIZZLE terms probably originated from restaurants that serve sizzling steaks that look, smell and sound better than they taste.

Stickiness

In banking, the tendency of credit rates to remain high longer than necessary when the cycle tops out. Hence, the phenomenon of credit rate *stickiness*. The same concept applies to company benefits indexed to economic cycles: on the reversal of a swing to the employee's benefit, *stickiness* of rates often applies.

Stick to your knitting

An outmoded rural expression that has found new life in the business world. Companies are increasingly advised to avoid excessive diversification, thus to *stick to their knitting*. Knitters apparently are good at concentrating on their efforts at the expense of everything else.

Stonewalling

Refusing to cooperate, as during a take-over attempt. A typical *stonewall* defence would be a firm stance against a PREDATOR, using every possible trick to turn him away including bluff and bluster. The PREDATOR eventually recognizes the *stonewall* as impenetrable, and looks elsewhere for prey.

Street smart

Effective in a tough, crude manner; using skills picked up in

Sticking to your knitting

the rough world of street fighting, or its figurative equivalent. A synonym is streetwise.

Stress flush

No, he is not just back from holiday, it is his inability to cope with stress that make him look sunburned. If the colouring doesn't go away at weekends, it is high blood pressure.

Strike price

In program trading, the price at which a bloc of stock will automatically be sold. Thousands of *strike prices* were hit in the week of 19 October 1987, aggravating the crash of the New York Stock Exchange. Markets in the rest of the free world followed.

Stroking

The care and feeding of employees to ensure a high level of

PSYCHIC INCOME. Also known as TLC, or Tender, Loving Care.

Suboptimization

Managing with gross self-interest. You are guilty of *suboptimization* if you take such a parochial view of your division that you ignore the greater good of the company's overall effort. By extension, mindless refusal to entertain the possibility of collaboration with other companies, even if benefits would accrue for all concerned.

Success fee

The bonus you pay your advisers when their strategy succeeds. In mergers and acquisition work, the *success fee* is often in the millions of dollars.

Sugging

Derived from Selling Under the Guise of market research. Insurance salesmen, for example, might detain you on the pretext of conducting a survey on accidents in the home, eventually pulling out the order book.

Suicide pill

A defence against PREDATORS that is so poisonous as to threaten the existence of the target company in the event of a take-over. (See also SHARK REPELLENT, POISON PILL.)

Suits

Blue-collar code language for white-collar managers. As in, 'Look busy. Here come the *suits*.'

Sunrise

The high technology industries that will drive tomorrow's economy. The opposite of SUNSET industries.

Sunset

The industries in decline, especially in the West: coal mining, steel, aluminium. The opposite of SUNRISE industries.

SWELL

YUPPIE talk, at least in London, that stands for 'Single Woman Earning Lots in London.' Probably meaningless anywhere else.

SWOT

An acronym for Strengths, Weaknesses, Opportunities and Threats, the framework for evaluating the prospects of a new product in the market-place.

Synergism

In the seventeenth century, a theological controversy over the combined effect of God's will and the human will. Synergists believed that both human and divine forces were at play in the conversion of sinners. Now a less controversial concept describing the bonus in output gained by the joint effort of groups of employees or disparate parts of an organization.

T

Tailgating

An American term for a stockbroker's decision to sell or buy on his own personal account in tune with the initiatives of one of his large investors. The expression comes from the habit of drivers who follow too closely the car ahead, in effect clinging to an estate car's tailgate. In market terms, sometimes just as dangerous.

Take no prisoners

A manager's exhortation to the troops, intended to appeal to the killer competitive instinct. Used mostly by Americans, the term calls for a spirit of ruthless single-mindedness. The idea is to leave rivals dead, not wounded.

Tax holiday

A specific period of tax relief granted to a company, usually as an incentive for investing in a region that needs employment. In Europe, countries, and regions within countries, compete with each other to attract outside investment. In the US, each state has its own charms and lures.

Technoid

A technically orientated person so involved in the marvels of technology that he/she seems only vaguely human, or HUMANOID. A hybrid of 'technology' and 'humanoid', the word is a successor to 'techie'. (See also COMPUTER NERD.)

Teething

The early obstacles to putting a new company on a steady

growth path. Finding the perfect management team might be a *teething* problem. Real teething, of course, is for babies.

Telephone numbers

A derisory term for excessively large salaries or outlandish prices paid for companies. By extension, any long string of numbers, so large it looks at first glance like a telephone number.

Texas handshake

A deal – usually American – made on the basis of trust and mutual understanding rather than by means of lengthy negotiation and a mountain of legal paperwork. Often employed in joint ventures that are undertaken as short-term arrangements to meet special requirements: a materials shortage, a shortfall in production capacity or a new opportunity in the marketplace. So-called because in Texas, a man's word is sacred, or so they say.

Theory K

The Korean management approach – results-orientated, more aggressive and more direct than the Japanese way.

Theory X

Management jargon for companies that function on the military model: centralized decision-making, rigid hierarchies, TOP-DOWN authority. Now a disappearing species.

Theory Y

The more humane, people-orientated management style that emerged in the 1980s, replacing THEORY X in many companies.

Theory Z

For those who couldn't make a success of THEORY X or THEORY Y, along came *Theory Z* in 1981, William Ouchi's interpretation of Japanese management techniques.

Therblig

A classification of 18 basic movements in manual work, identified by motion specialist Frank Gilbreth. Developed early in this century, the system is still used. Each of the 18 movements (such as search, select and assemble) is called a 'therblig', which is Gilbreth spelled approximately backward.

Threadneedler

An official of the Bank of England, located in Threadneedle Street in London.

Throwing money (at problems)

The simplistic solution for a business unit's problems: give in to a complaining manager and allocate more resources to him or her. In extreme cases, the additional funds come so fast that the money seems to be thrown. Yet rarely can weakness be corrected with indiscriminate injections of capital. What goes away is only the money, not the problem.

Throw it at the wall, see if it sticks

A well-known technique in Italian cuisine to test how thoroughly the pasta is cooked (if it sticks, it's ready to eat). Now also a marketing term for trying out an idea with a client, or in public. The expression succeeds 'Run it up the flagpole'.

Tidbytes

Cutesy jargon from computer industry writers who try to

Throw it at the wall . . . see if it sticks

appropriate legitimate words from the English language and infuse them with local colour. In this case, 'tidbits' has been corrupted to signify snippets of information about computers.

Title inflation

Good news – you are promoted to vice president sooner than your friends. The salary increase was minimal, but the prestige makes up for that. But hang on, here's the bad news: within a year, all your friends are also vice presidents, also with little or no more money attached. You are all victims of *title inflation*, where the concept, rather than the currency, is cheapened. Next round: you all become senior vice presidents.

Tombstone

Financial advertising mandatory in some countries to make public the participants in underwritings or other major transactions. So called because of the grey, sombre design encased in a funereal black border.

Top-down

A management style, now in disrepute, that works along military lines. The generals bark orders down the chain of command and subordinates obey, no questions asked. In the 1980s, Western companies began to realize that workers not only resented being ordered about, they actually had constructive ideas to offer.

Top-of-the-line

The most expensive, usually the most profitable, product in your range. At General Motors, Cadillac is the *top of the line*, and profit per car is high compared to the bottom of the line. In New York, pronounced 'toppuda-line'.

Top out

The point at which a performance curve reaches its highest level, and prepares to turn downward. The opposite of BOTTOM OUT.

Track record

A BUZZWORD from the sporting world, where runners, horses and cars establish their level of competitiveness by a history of their finishing times. A fitting metaphor for business, where a *track record* implies a picture of consistent performance at peak effort.

Transparent

Computer and communications systems so well adapted to

human needs that working with them in no way slows your thought processes. Thus the machines become *transparent*, if not invisible.

Trickle-down theory

The key element of Reaganomics and its European variations, which boldly promises that making the rich richer through easier taxation will eventually help all levels of society. The theory holds that the rich will spend more, stimulating the economy and allowing the prosperity to 'trickle down' through the lower strata of society. In most cases where the system has been attempted, the rich get richer, but the rest is never clear.

Turf

Your territory, the place you draw the line in *turf* battles, the things you think of when you become *turf*-conscious, the areas you keep colleagues out of when they threaten your space.

The Twelve

Euro-shorthand for the 12 members of the European Community: France, Germany, Britain, Italy, Ireland, Belgium, the Netherlands, Luxembourg, Denmark, Greece, Spain and Portugal.

U

Unbundling

Separating a package of products or services so that its components can be sold separately, usually at a considerably higher aggregate price.

Unmentionables

Products that ordinary people resent seeing advertised, on grounds of bad taste. Obviously a problem for some manufacturing companies. The *unmentionables* include over-the-counter ointments for haemorrhoids, female hygiene products, mortuary services and constipation remedies. The taste threshold varies widely from country to country.

Up and running

Mainly a computer industry term to identify the point at which the system is actually working as designed to.

Upfront

American slang for being candid and honest from the outset. An *upfront* person is one who will often tell you more than you want to know about him/herself.

Upload

Jargon for 'send', as in transmitting words or numbers from one computer to another. The term has been forced upon the public by computer software makers, who have a bizarre vocabulary all their own. (See also DOWNLOAD.)

Upmarket

A British term for the higher end of the market. 'Moving *upmarket*' with your product, or your child's school, means leaving one class and climbing the ladder to the next. It is a slippery path. (See also DOWNMARKET.)

Upside/downside

The two sides of a risk–reward formula in which the possible gains are said to be the *upside* of the performance line, and the possible losses the *downside*. Not to be confused with 'upside-down'.

Upstream

The stages of a manufacturing process that precede your company's activity. If you assemble gumball machines, the manufacture of all the parts, and the extraction of raw materials for those parts, are *upstream* from you. Distribution and marketing are DOWNSTREAM.

Upward communicator

An ambitious, career-minded young executive contemptuous of his equals or inferiors but eager to please and serve those above him. A dangerous game, as those abused on the way up the ladder may be encountered again on the way down.

User-friendly

A description of computer software that attempts to calm the fears of the COMPUTER-SHY. Software makers want to attract users who find computers overtly unfriendly, even hostile. By extension any product that the seller wishes to propose as easy to use. Don't believe it.

V

VALS

Market research acronym for 'Values And Life Styles', a classification of personality types to help advertisers focus on segments of the population. There are nine subdivisions, ranging from the bottom type, the 'survivor', to the top, the 'integrated' consumer.

Value added

The enhancement of a product's or material's value during the manufacturing process. In services, the *value added* might be the expertise contributed to a strategy by a team of consultants.

Vaporware

Products in the software industry that are announced prematurely. Many 'vaporize' because of development problems.

Vertical integration

The incorporation of businesses directly related, UPSTREAM or DOWNSTREAM, to your product. A restaurateur who buys a duck farm is practising *vertical integration*.

Vulture capitalist

A venture capitalist who takes advantage of an entrepreneur by structuring deals so that the entrepreneur benefits very little from the success but the investors get rich. The moral justification of such investors is that the entrepreneur is only in love with the idea; financial gain is secondary.

Vulture capitalist

V-word

Shorthand for 'vision', one of the faddish panaceas for
executives who are floundering in the practice of management. *V-word* would most likely be used mockingly by the
executive's subordinates, who know he has none. In such circumstances, the word becomes too fearsome to pronounce
aloud. By extension, office wits will often create other unpro-
nounceables on an ad hoc basis. In a company heading for
liquidation, for example, they may caution against using the
L-word. In a company struggling to catch up with competitors' technology, and failing, they would avoid mentioning
the T-word.

W

Walking wounded

The men and women whose business lives have been disrupted or destroyed by forces beyond their control. They find it hard to believe their loyalty and diligence have brought them such grief. Recognizable by their despondent shuffle and vacant stare. With the coming rationalization of European industry under the 1992 programme, the *walking wounded* are sure to be a common feature of Europe's business landscape.

Wannabe

Sometimes written as 'Wannabee' this term describes the young person whose sights are set two or three jobs up the career ladder. Everything he or she does is designed to clear the way for the next promotion. These people talk mostly about what they 'want to be', not what they are supposed to be contributing today. A more aggressive variant is the super self-confident 'Gonnabe'.

War cabinet

A company's inner circle of top managers, accountants, lawyers and other strategists convened as a temporary team to fight off unwanted attention from outside, as from PREDATORS in a take-over battle. (If you are not in the *war cabinet*, you are probably not IN THE LOOP.) Perhaps an overblown metaphor, but not really out of place. Real warfare differs from a take-over fight only in terms of scale and in the use of live ammunition.

War chest

A company's available funds for a major market-place struggle or investment, usually unfriendly.

War room

An office or suite of offices for planning a major, prolonged defensive or offensive action. In his take-over battle for Société Générale de Belgique, Carlo De Benedetti took an entire floor of the Brussels Hilton as his *war room*. The WAR CABINET usually lives there for the duration of the struggle.

Wash

In accounting, an item of revenue that is exactly offset by an expense. The *wash* is the effect of one hand washing the other.

Wash-trade

Stock market jargon for the short-term purchase and sale of a company's stock so as to give the impression of trading activity, thereby driving up the price. As the price climbs, the original *wash-traders* all pull out, leaving other investors holding the bag. A kind of CONCERT PARTY; may be illegal in your country.

Wastage

See ATTRITION.

Watch list

A list of under-performing employees under special scrutiny. Also a financial term for a listing of securities that exhibit unusual patterns of performance. In such cases, the *watch list* is monitored by the market authorities.

Weltanschauung

A German term creeping into English, *Weltanschauung* simply means 'world view'. In business, it is used in the sense of a company's attitude towards the competitive scene. Literally, *Welt* (world) *Anschauung* (perception).

What-if

Games people play on computer spreadsheets to test variables in their business plans. 'Let's play *what-if* with prices,' says the MBA-trained planner. He wants to see the impact of different pricing on profitability, tax exposure or competitive positioning. 'Let's play *what-if* with the payroll,' he says. What he wants to see is how big reductions in personnel can improve the bottom line.

Whistle-blower

An employee who informs the civil or criminal authorities of his company's illegal activities. Such people rarely keep their jobs.

White-collar scrap

The time and energy wasted in service industries or administrative jobs that fail to add value to the end product. Coined by Michael Hessick, of Robert E. Nolan Co., this term describes one of the great problems of our time — measuring white-collar productivity. The *'scrap'*, if you could see it, would make an impressive heap in most companies. Manufacturers have ways of eliminating such waste. The white-collar variety is harder to trap.

White knight

In a hostile take-over battle, a company that offers to outbid

Whistle blower

the original PREDATOR on the promise of being a more accept-
able master to the take-over target company. In its role as
saviour, it becomes the mythical knight in shining armour of
fairy tales. Often about as realistic a concept.

Wiggle room

Latitude, or elbow room, that you should build into your
plan, your strategy or your life to allow some freedom of
action when trouble develops. An executive without *wiggle
room* is a prisoner of his/her pronouncements. A manager
who is forced to agree to unrealistic profit targets will suffer
from an uncomfortable shortage of same.

Winding down

A euphemism for closing or dismantling a plant or a business.

Nothing is ever wound partially down. Sort of the opposite of winding up.

Window

Global business jargon for the few hours a day in which customers or colleagues far away are awake or in the office at the same time you are. Global traders in money and other commodities open the *window* wider by keeping their offices staffed at all hours of the day and night. Expatriates working a continent away from home learn to use the *window* to their advantage.

Window of opportunity

In any business, it is the timing that makes the difference. The *window* is a space metaphor for the opening in time during which an initiative can be taken. For businessmen who have trouble thinking in the abstract, this kind of expression brings the idea into clearer focus.

Win/win

A negotiating stance in which one party attempts to find a solution that both parties can feel good about. Women managers are said to excel at this. The opposite of the more standard 'win/lose' approach of the male negotiator in which one side attempts to squeeze the other for every possible drop of blood.

Workaholic

A person suffering from a need to demonstrate a devotion to work. Psychologists believe that a tendency to overwork can mask various fears and loathings, including such basics as going home at a reasonable hour to join the family. Alcoholism is more destructive, but *workaholism* is right up there.

World class

A level of competence great enough to ensure survival in open international competition. Originally a sporting term ('world class sprinter'), but now increasingly applied to companies as a measure of their competitiveness. US author Richard Schonberger used it to describe a range of industrial practices in his 1987 book *World Class Manufacturing*.

WYSIWYG

Pronounce it 'wizzy-wig' if you must use it, but try to find a synonym for this new capability of desktop publishing systems to display a page on a computer screen before printing it. The term is inside slang for 'What You See Is What You Get'.

X

X-factor

That mysterious, undefinable something in a person or a company that brings success. As long as it remains an *X-factor*, it cannot be copied by the competition. The late novelist Vladimir Nabokov once wrote that success is determined by three factors: heredity, environment and ingredient x. And ingredient x, he added, is by far the most important.

Y

Young old

Marketing jargon for consumers in the 55–75 age group. Certain sales campaigns, for such items as false-teeth adhesive and energising medicines, are aimed at this group.

Yuppie

An extended acronym for Young Urban Professional. This individual was discovered by market researchers delving into the habits of young adults in the 1980s. *Yuppies* are FAST-TRACK performers who make so much money so fast that they often come down with AFFLUENZA.

Z

Zaitech

Creeping daily into the language of international finance, this hybrid word from Japan combines *zaimu* (Japanese for finance) with *technology* to produce a trendy term for the technique of earning profits from a company's investments rather than from sales.

Zapping

Fast forwarding or muting a video-recorded version of a television programme to avoid having to watch the commercials. A source of great worry to television advertisers.

Zero-base budgeting

The most difficult, but often the most intelligent, approach to budgeting. Each line is calculated on the basis of real need rather than as a multiple of last year's numbers. This forces managers to rethink their spending with each new budget period.

Zero defects

That elusive target in operations striving for perfect-quality output.

Zero sum

In GAME THEORY, the solution in which the losses and the gains are a WASH.

Zilch

A US expression of unknown origin meaning 'zero' or 'nothing'. Americans use it when they want to add flair or emphasis to a declaration, as in, 'My margins in the market are *zilch*.' A synonym is ZIP.

Zip

See ZILCH.